LIBRARY

# Primary Languages in Practice

# Primary Languages in Practice

## A Guide to Teaching and Learning

Jane Jones and Angela McLachlan

 Open University Press

Open University Press
McGraw-Hill Education
McGraw-Hill House
Shoppenhangers Road
Maidenhead
Berkshire
England
SL6 2QL

email: enquiries@openup.co.uk
world wide web: www.openup.co.uk

and

Two Penn Plaza, New York, NY 10121-2289, USA

First published 2009

Copyright © Jane Jones and Angela McLachlan 2009

A catalogue record of this book is available from the British Library

ISBN10: 0 335 23532 8 (pb) 0335 23533 6 (hb)
ISBN13: 978 0 335 23532 2 (pb) 978 0335 23533 9 (hb)

Library of Congress Cataloging-in-Publication Data
CIP data has been applied for

Typeset by Aptara Inc., India
Printed in the UK by Bell and Bain Ltd., Glasgow

Fictitious names of companies, products, people, characters and/or data that may be used herein (in case studies or in examples) are not intended to represent any real individual, company, product or event.

Mixed Sources
Product group from well-managed
forests and other controlled sources
www.fsc.org Cert no. TT-COC-002769
© 1996 Forest Stewardship Council

# Contents

*Foreword*                                                                         vii
*Preface*                                                                           ix
*Acknowledgements*                                                                 xiii
*About the authors*                                                                 xv
*List of acronyms*                                                                xvii

**Introduction**
Primary languages in practice: an integrated approach to teaching
and learning                                                                         1

 1  Primary languages: past and present                                              6

 2  Becoming a primary languages practitioner                                       17

 3  Effective planning in primary languages                                         31

 4  Teaching and learning strategies for the classroom                              60

 5  Monitoring, assessing and recording progress in primary languages:
    an AfL approach to primary languages                                            82

 6  The role of the primary languages subject leader                               100

 7  Planning for continuity and progression: transition from KS2 to KS3            116

 8  The role of the school-based subject mentor                                     131

 9  In the field: from theory to practice                                          145

10  Learning abroad: teacher professional placements and school trips              160

Epilogue: the primary languages teacher as researcher                              176

*Appendix: key websites*                                                           180
*Bibliography*                                                                      182
*Index*                                                                             187

# Foreword

The introduction of the National Languages Strategy could not have been more timely. Recent economic developments have reminded us that, as a country, we have to compete in an increasingly competitive and challenging international context. An awareness of the lifestyles, cultures and, indeed, languages of those from other communities is, therefore, essential for our next generation of citizens.

At the same time, introducing the teaching of languages into primary schools is a major curriculum reform that will require careful implementation if it is to succeed. Inevitably, the attitudes, skills and practices of teachers will be crucial factors in pulling this off. This being the case, the task must be to develop contexts within which teachers feel supported as well as challenged in relation to their responsibility to keep exploring more effective ways of facilitating the language learning of all of their children. This, in turn, has major implications for school organization and leadership.

This new book makes a significant contribution to such reform efforts. Written by two authors who have a deep understanding of what language learning among primary age children involves, it provides a rich range of resources that teachers and schools will find valuable as they take on the challenge of this curriculum reform. In so doing, the book addresses an impressive range of relevant issues regarding what effective practice involves and how it can be fostered. The authors wisely position their discussion of these issues in the context of overall school improvement efforts, the changes that are occurring in the primary curriculum, and overall national policies, not least the Every Child Matters agenda.

A strong feature of the book is the way it relates theory to practice. At the same time, the authors are realistic in explaining and responding to the many practical challenges that still have to be faced. Here the frequent use of accounts of practice, and worked examples of lesson plans and teaching materials will be particularly helpful to readers as they consider how to move forward.

While the main focus of the book is on language learning, its agenda has, I believe, much wider implications for the work of schools. The ideas that are explored are about making teaching and learning effective across the curriculum, not least in relation to oracy and literacy. It is hardly surprising, therefore, that the text explores important aspects of effective practice, such as the use of assessment for learning, and strategies for developing practice through school-based staff development activities. In this way the authors argue for a whole-school approach to primary languages provision. The vision they offer is one that demands cultural change within our primary schools. And, of course, cultural change requires effective leadership.

So, this book offers both a set of challenges and a source of practical support in addressing these challenges. As such, it deserves to be widely read and used.

**Mel Ainscow**
**Professor of Education**
**University of Manchester**

# Preface

Modern Languages have become part of the mainstream primary school curriculum for learners at Key Stage 2 (KS2), 7–11 year olds in the United Kingdom, and thus the entitlement for these children to learn a language other than English has become a reality. The pre- and in-service teachers who are being trained to deliver this entitlement, and who will have a considerable responsibility for the development of language teaching and learning in the primary curriculum, need ongoing support to help them take on their task confidently in the short term, and with vision for the longer term. This book aims to provide support to enable these teachers to develop as effective practitioners and to embed best practice in their language programmes in primary schools.

In writing this book, we have sought to offer an informed framework of professional development for primary practitioners in both initial and continuing teacher education. We have situated languages firmly in the primary curriculum, which is what we consider to be central to the longer-term national vision for, and ultimate success of, primary languages. Trainers, Local Authority Advisers, headteachers, school governors and classroom teachers will find many points of reference to support their development of primary languages programmes. Secondary languages trainees and teachers will find it an invaluable reference for understanding the context of primary languages, and for planning effective transition.

There are a number of features throughout the book which demonstrate 'real-world' experience of primary languages practice. These include:

- *Teachers talking*: illustrative case studies of effective school practice
- *Trainees talking*: trainees' reflections and perspectives
- *Pupils talking*: pupils' perspectives and samples of pupils' work
- *Primary languages in practice*: samples of key items of documentation, for example, school language policies, language teaching observation reports, lesson plans; practical whole- and small-group activities
- *Reflective practice in action*: reflective whole- and small-group training activities
- *Exploring primary languages*: websites, useful references, further reading and other related links.

While there is some focus on specialist primary languages training programmes, we also provide useful guidance for those on general Primary PGCE programmes, as well as for trainers and other providers who work in primary education. Whilst emphasizing the importance of the initial training experience of teachers as a crucial formative experience, we consider that a successful languages provision goes beyond the single classroom of the specialist languages teacher. It extends to multiple classrooms where class teachers and teaching assistants, with the support of the Headteacher, contribute to the provision, and indeed to the whole school community where the non-teaching staff, governors and parents have a role to play in supporting and ensuring rich and coherent language learning opportunities. For this reason, this book takes a whole-school and school community perspective on primary languages provision, and we have tried to create a book that can act as an anchor text to provide useful information, and practical support and ideas for all those involved.

Our book is structured in a logical sequence but with much looping backwards and forwards. This reflects our view of language learning in the classroom as cyclical and consolidatory as well as essentially progression-focused. We have included as many practical examples and snap shots of practice as space would allow, drawing on material and ideas we have developed and evaluated ourselves, as well as from imaginative primary practitioners in schools with effective primary practice. We have had many conversations with teachers, tutors, trainees, both from the UK and overseas, and pupils about the issues we have encountered and identified as pivotal in ensuring successful, long-term national programmes of primary languages, and we include selections from these conversations.

## Overview

We begin with a brief introduction about the aims of primary languages as these have evolved since the advent of the National Languages Strategy (NLaS; DfES 2002b), and how its overarching objectives correspond to the renewed Primary National Strategy. Chapter 2 discusses the professional profile of the primary languages practitioner, situating practice within the canon of effective primary practice as a whole. In Chapter 3, we look closely at how to plan for meaningful teaching and learning in the short, medium and long term, and how to ensure that language learning both integrates into, and supports, learning across the curriculum. Chapter 4 explores a range of teaching strategies that ensure sound and inclusive practice, with a particular focus on the development of literacy and oracy skills, and embedding languages into classroom routines. We consider assessment as essentially formative and integral to learning and teaching and Chapter 5 emphasizes an Assessment for Learning (AfL) approach in monitoring and progressing learning and in supporting effective planning. It is important for schools to have a workable assessment policy that includes feasible and useful recording tools. The role of the Primary Languages Subject Leader is the focus of Chapter 6. Leadership is important in any subject but acutely so in the primary languages community that is still developing its subject identity. We assert the need for well-informed subject leadership that is part of a shared construct based on teamwork and collaboration within the school and on a cross-phase basis.

Primary language provision cannot be entirely successful or sustainable without effective and practical transition to KS3 at secondary level. Chapter 7 is concerned with key aspects of transition and ways to enhance the 'bridges' between phases to ensure learning progression and coherence of teaching provision. We emphasize how important it is for primary and secondary languages teachers to understand each other's practice. Chapter 8 evolves naturally from Chapter 7, and suggests ways to develop the crucial role of the school-based subject mentor, which in other curriculum areas is central to programmes of ITE, as well as mentorship of newly qualified teachers (NQTs).

Both the subject leader, and subject mentor, have been identified by Ofsted (2008) as areas that are in urgent need of development. We move on in Chapter 9 to outlining how trainees, with the support of well-informed mentors, can develop good practice during their school placements, and in Chapter 10, we explore the potential of the overseas professional placement, not only in providing professional learning in the context of primary languages practice, with a particular emphasis on opportunities for language and cultural learning in international contexts, but also in enhancing the overall professional development and practice of beginning primary practitioners. We look at arranging and exploiting the trainee teachers' period of study abroad and the experiences involved in one of the hallmarks of the entire language learning enterprise, a school trip abroad.

The epilogue concludes the book but opens the way to continuing professional learning and to developing the teacher's research role in the community of practice. The languages teacher is a lifelong learner *par excellence* needing constantly to update linguistic and cultural knowledge. Adopting the stance of teacher researcher into classroom practices will enable the teacher to understand better and to enhance and develop the quality of the language learning experience.

We, the authors, are subject leaders in language teacher education in university Departments of Education and between us cover the primary and secondary phases, as well as being active researchers in the field, both nationally and internationally. We bring to this volume a wealth of expertise, passion for the early language learning enterprise and a belief in sound, well-planned and imaginative training to ensure effectiveness of provision. Our own experiences of language teaching and learning and our many engagements with other cultures underpin our commitment to developing challenging and effective language teachers, specialist or otherwise, who can contribute significantly to children's primary school learning experiences and their enjoyment in learning.

# Acknowledgements

With thanks to our family, friends and colleagues who, as ever, have given invaluable support during the writing of this book. A special mention to the Head, Deputy Head, staff, pupils and parents of Elmridge Primary School, who have consistently supported all our ideas, answered all our questions, and contributed enormously to our understanding of the reality of primary languages teaching and learning.

# About the authors

**Jane Jones** is Head of MFL Teacher Education and Senior Lecturer in Education in the Department of Education and Professional Studies at King's College London. She is subject leader for the PGCE Secondary course and for the MA in MFL Education. Trained as a primary-secondary teacher, she taught MFL in several comprehensive schools in London and the South East and assisted with primary languages provision in state primary and prep schools.

Jane was deputy director of the DfES 2004 national research project into primary languages provision and has reported on transition arrangements for LAs. Jane has been filmed for CILT (the Centre for Information on Language Teaching/The National Centre for Languages) for training programmes. She has been UK coordinator of many international research projects on issues concerned with early language learning and with comparative education. Her research interests include primary-secondary transition, comparative education and especially Assessment for Learning. Key publications include *Modern Foreign Languages 5–11: Guidelines for Teachers* (with Simon Coffey for Routledge) and *MFL inside the Black Box* (with Dylan Wiliam for GL Assessment, London).

**Angela McLachlan** is the Course Leader for Modern Languages in the Primary PGCE and Teach First programmes in the School of Education, University of Manchester. She has worked in CPD, and in primary, secondary and adult language teaching and language teacher education, both in the UK and overseas. She has recently been involved in an EU-funded language teacher training project, focusing on the use of new communication technologies in language teaching and learning. She has published a language resource book, *French in the Primary Classroom: Ideas and Resources for Teachers* (Continuum, 2009), and is also working on a French language course for primary teachers *Teach Yourself French for Primary Teachers* (Hodder & Stoughton, forthcoming). Key research publications include *Modern languages in the primary curriculum: are we creating conditions for success?* (Language Learning Journal) and *Bringing Modern Languages into the Primary Curriculum in England: Investigating Effective Practice in Teacher Education* (European Journal of Teacher Education).

# List of acronyms

| | |
|---|---|
| AfL | Assessment for Learning |
| ALL | Association for Language Learning |
| AT | Attainment Target |
| CEF(R) | Common European Framework of Reference |
| CEPD | Career Entry Development Profile |
| CILT | Centre for Information on Language Teaching, now The National Centre for Languages |
| CoE | Council of Europe |
| CPD | Continuing Professional Development |
| CRF | Common Reference Framework |
| DCSF | Department for Children, Schools and Families (formerly DfES) |
| EAL | English as an Additional Language |
| ECM | Every Child Matters |
| ECML | European Centre for Modern Languages |
| ELL | Early Language Learning |
| ELP | European Languages Portfolio |
| ETML | Early Teaching of Modern Languages |
| FLA | Foreign Languages Assistant |
| G&T | Gifted and Talented |
| HEI | Higher Education Institution |
| HMI | Her Majesty's Inspector |
| HoD | Head of Department |
| ITE | Initial Teacher Education |
| ITTMFL | Initial Teacher Training in Modern Foreign Languages |
| IWB | Interactive Whiteboard |
| KS2 | Key Stage 2 |
| KS3 | Key Stage 3 |
| KAL | Knowledge About Language |
| LA | Local Authority |
| LEA | Local Education Authority |
| LL | Languages Ladder |
| LLS | language learning strategies |
| LO | Learning Objective or Outcome |
| LSA | Learning Support Assistant |
| MFL | Modern Foreign Languages |
| ML | Modern Languages |
| NACELL | The National Advisory Centre for Early Language Learning |
| NC | National Curriculum |
| NLaS | National Languages Strategy |
| NQT | Newly Qualified Teacher |

PGCE  Postgraduate Certificate in Education
PMFL  Primary Modern Foreign Languages
PPA  Planning, Preparation and Assessment
QCA  Qualifications and Curriculum Authority
QTS  Qualified Teacher Status
SEN  Special Educational Needs
SIP  School Improvement Plan
SLA  Second Language Acquisition
SLC  Specialist Language College
SoW  Scheme of Work
T & L  Teaching and Learning
TA  Teaching Assistant
TDA  Training and Development Agency for Schools.
TL  Target Language (i.e. the language being taught)
TTA  Teacher Training Agency
VAK  Visual, Auditory, Kinesthetic
VC  Videoconferencing
WB  Whiteboard

# Introduction

## Primary languages in practice: an integrated approach to teaching and learning

> Every child should have the opportunity throughout KS2 to study a foreign language and develop their interest in the culture of other nations. They should have access to high quality teaching and learning opportunities, making use of native speakers and e-learning. By age 11 they should have the opportunity to reach a recognized level of competence on the Common European Framework and for that achievement to be recognized through a national scheme. The KS2 language learning programme must include at least one of the working languages of the European Union and be delivered at least in part in class time.
>
> (National Languages Strategy, DfES 2002b: 15)

The National Languages Strategy (NLaS), published in 2002, set out a clear vision for early language learning in England as the first steps in a process of lifelong language learning. But for primary languages to succeed, we must ensure that it becomes an integral and symbiotic element of the primary curriculum itself, creating a synergy of learning across the curriculum as a whole. For this to happen, we must view its provision with an equal robustness to that of other areas of the curriculum. Sir Jim Rose, writing in the *Independent Review of the Primary Curriculum* (DCSF 2008: 61) points to the role of primary languages in contributing to children's 'cultural understanding, language and literacy skills, and strategies and dispositions for learning generally', clearly underlining the potential benefits of robust primary languages programmes. We would argue that where primary languages remain marginalized, delivered by a teaching community lacking in subject knowledge and subject-specific pedagogy, it is doubtful whether real integration, and thus *acceptance* of, and *belief* in, its role in children's learning will remain anything but superficial.

### Synergy in learning: the Primary National Curriculum, the Primary National Strategy and the KS2 Framework for Languages

So what is the primary curriculum currently seeking to achieve? In the *National Curriculum: Handbook for Primary Teachers in England* (DfES 2002a), the DfES expressed its *aims* as follows:

- the school curriculum should aim to provide opportunities for all pupils to learn and achieve;
- the school curriculum should aim to promote pupils' spiritual, moral, social and cultural development, and prepare all pupils for the opportunities, responsibilities and experiences of life.

Its *purposes* are given as:

- to establish an entitlement ... to develop knowledge, understanding, skills and attitudes necessary for their self-fulfilment and development as active and responsible citizens;
- to establish standards ... to set targets for improvement, measure progress towards those targets, and monitor and compare performance between individuals, groups and schools;
- to promote continuity and coherence ... that promotes curriculum continuity [and] ... facilitates the transition of pupils between schools and phases of education and provides a foundation of lifelong learning;
- to promote public understanding ... of, and confidence in ... the learning and achievements resulting from compulsory education.

It recognizes that

> The curriculum itself cannot remain static. It must be responsive to changes in society and the economy, and changes in the nature of schooling itself. Teachers, individually and collectively, have to reappraise their teaching in response to the changing needs of their pupils and the impact of economic, social and cultural change. Education only flourishes if it successfully adapts to the demands and needs of the time.
>
> (DfES 2002a: 13)

This is a key message for primary practitioners, and the primary community as a whole: the curriculum must be iteratively reviewed and evaluated, and changes identified as central to the aims and purposes of the curriculum as a whole will, *de facto*, require that the professional knowledge and skills of teachers are likewise reviewed, evaluated and developed to meet the demands of those changes. As Hopkins et al. (1994: 66) commented, 'teaching and learning are the prime focus of school improvement efforts' and they concluded that, 'teacher development [lies] at the heart of school improvement efforts' (1994: 60).

Macrory and McLachlan (2009) discussed the issue of developing the skills base of primary practitioners to include languages, as opposed to simply redeploying secondary practitioners in primary schools, commenting that,

> This solution calls into wider question the distinctions in the skills base of primary generalists and secondary languages subject specialists: are the latter equipped with the necessary knowledge and skills to teach a significantly

different age group, and is their understanding of the wider primary curriculum sufficient to enable them to adopt a truly cross-curricular approach to their teaching?

Indeed, Driscoll, Jones and Macrory (2004: 11) also found a clear preference for languages to be taught by primary school staff. Developing teacher knowledge in this way is, in our view, the only way to ensure that primary languages are embedded in the canon of primary practice.

Certainly, in terms of whole school improvement, we would argue that the integrated curriculum has to be embraced by, and embedded in, the consciousness of the whole school, that is, staff, pupils, parents and governors. Our view of the importance of the role of the primary languages subject leader has its roots in the philosophy espoused by Hopkins et al. that effective schools, and thus, for us, effective learning, are characterized by a culture of collaboration. In the seven years since the inclusion of languages in the primary curriculum was first announced, progress towards real integration has been slow, and most schools still rely on sole practitioners. To succeed, to ensure effective learning, staff must collaborate, and work together to develop modes of practice that truly bring languages into the heart of the curriculum.

The past few years have seen a considerable amount of new policy in the primary phase, with increasing guidance on how these new policies complement each other. The advent of *Excellence and Enjoyment: A Strategy for Primary Schools* (DfES 2003), designed 'to help teachers and schools to raise standards across the whole curriculum', with a greater emphasis on creativity, personalized and independent learning, underlines the role of the National Languages Strategy within the Primary National Strategy as a whole, and provides primary practitioners with detailed guidance on the national vision for teaching and learning in the primary phase. This guidance was supplemented by the publication, in 2004, of *Every Child Matters: Change for Children* (DfES 2004a), which sought to promote a 'new approach to the well-being of children and young people from birth to age 19', and cited five key aims:

- Be healthy.
- Stay safe.
- Enjoy and achieve.
- Make a positive contribution.
- Achieve economic well-being.

Thus, a national framework for the *education* of children and young people is now formally complemented by a framework for their emotional and physical *well-being*, and the development of skills that will enable them to operate effectively in the economy. Increasing language competence, both in the first language – supported by the renewed literacy framework – and in a second language – supported by the KS2 Framework for

Languages, and the new programme of study at KS3, is seen as a key skill towards ensuring competitiveness in the home and global economies.

The renewal of the primary frameworks shifts emphasis from *teaching* objectives to *learning* objectives, with an increased focus on progress towards assessment for learning, as we argue forcefully in this book, building on Jones' research into assessment for learning in the context of language teaching and learning (Jones 2010; Jones and Wiliam 2008). The KS2 Framework for Languages, with its five key strands of literacy, oracy, intercultural understanding, knowledge about language and language learning strategies, and its focus on progressive learning objectives, sits well with the vision for learning encompassed within the primary national curriculum.

## A continuum of language learning

We would argue that the most important issue in conceptualizing a national programme of primary languages teaching and learning is that we must avoid the temptation of merely simplifying secondary languages teaching and learning. We need to think of language learning in terms of a *continuum* of language learning, not in discrete language learning 'stages', an issue raised by Muijs et al. in 2005, Jones in 2005 and again by McLachlan in 2009b. A continuum of learning by definition reinforces the notion of *lifelong learning* in which compulsory education plays only a beginning role, and resonates with both the vision of the NLaS, and the National Primary Strategy. The aims of the new secondary curriculum, introduced in September 2008, resonate with those of the primary curriculum, and seek to create:

- Successful learners, who enjoy learning, make progress and achieve.
- Confident individuals who are able to live safe, healthy and fulfilling lives.
- Responsible citizens who make a positive contribution to society.

The new programme of study for languages at KS3, as part of the new secondary curriculum, goes some way to building on primary learning in general, and language learning in particular. It conceptualizes language learning as part of a lifelong process, concerned with an enriched and cohesive curriculum, and a focus on creativity, flexibility, independent learning and an increased understanding and acceptance of cultural diversity.

For more information on the new secondary curriculum, consult: www.curriculum.qca.org.uk.

## Conclusion

As we argue above, and elsewhere in the book, achieving success in primary languages rests on the wider acceptance of languages as a core part of the curriculum, in developing teacher knowledge and skills, and in ensuring a real progression in learning. Against a backdrop of concern for the 'loss of childhood' as expressed by Alexander (2008), successful primary language experiences can contribute to joyful childhood learning and engender empowered active learners. The feedback from primary pupils about their early language learning is overwhelmingly positive, their enjoyment tangible, their agency and achievement considerable, providing a strong Every Child Matters (ECM) cornerstone upon which to build.

# 1 Primary languages

## Past and present

This chapter discusses:

- developments in language teaching in England from the early 1960s
- the landmark 'French from Eight' scheme conducted by Burstall et al. and its impact upon subsequent schemes
- the National Languages Strategy and its implications for primary practitioners
- the current picture in primary languages.

## From Burstall to the National Languages Strategy

The ability to understand and communicate in other languages is increasingly important in our society and in the global economy. Languages contribute to the cultural and linguistic richness of our society, to personal fulfilment, mutual understanding, commercial success and international trade and global citizenship. Our vision is clear – we must provide an opportunity for early language learning to harness children's learning potential and enthusiasm; we must provide high quality teaching and learning opportunities in the world of travel and work; we must provide opportunities for lifelong language learning; we must recognize language skills as central to breaking down barriers both within this country and between our nation and others. This is why we must transform our country's capability in languages.
(Catherine Ashton, in *Languages for All: Languages for Life – A Strategy for England*, DfES 2002b)

This national vision for lifelong language learning, defined by Catherine Ashton in the National Languages Strategy (DfES 2002b), coupled with both the educational and intercultural benefits it can bring, has evolved over a significant period of time. For a full understanding of the time that it is taking for primary languages to become an integrated part of the primary curriculum when so many other countries have prioritized early language learning, it is important to locate primary languages in educational developments over the past 50 years. The 1960s saw primary education – hitherto known as 'elementary education' – gain prominence in the national awareness, emerging as a 'major and largely distinct sector' (Simon 1991). The structure of secondary education was firmly in the spotlight with the gradual move towards 'comprehensive' education and in August 1963 the then Secretary of State for Education, Sir Edward Boyle, reconstituted the Central Advisory Council to 'consider primary education in all its aspects and the transition to secondary school' (Simon 1991). It is interesting to note that 'transition' from primary into secondary education, which was to become one of the key factors working against the introduction of modern languages into the primary curriculum, was already at this stage identified as an area of enormous importance across the entire curriculum.

Earlier that year, Boyle had announced the launching of a 'Pilot Scheme to test the feasibility of starting French from the age of eight in state primary schools' (Hawkins 1996: 155). This scheme followed large-scale initiatives in the teaching of both science and mathematics 'on the wave of the curriculum reform movement which had its inception in the modernizing tendencies of the late 1950s' (Simon 1991: 314).

Until that time, the study of modern languages had effectively been the preserve of the grammar schools or the independent sector, with secondary modern education lagging lamentably behind. Indeed, until the mid-1960s, 'basic competence' in a modern language had been a standard entrance requirement to university (Hawkins 1996). As the global economy evolved, the rationale for teaching and learning languages began to change. Stenhouse noted in 1975:

> The origins of the schools' interest in the teaching of languages lie in the teaching of Latin (and to a lesser extent Greek), first as the *lingua franca* of the mediaeval scholarly world and later as a 'discipline to thought' and for the sake of classical literature. Modern languages were at first alternative disciplines for thinking and are now increasingly seen in practical terms.
>
> (1975: 12)

In 1963, the Nuffield Foundation commissioned a survey (Lazaro 1963) on the extent of modern language teaching in State schools. It found that 58 Local Education Authorities (LEAs) in England and Scotland reported that

> a foreign language had been introduced or would be introduced before the end of the session 1962/3, 200 schools in England and 80 in Scotland being involved. However only eighteen of the 58 LEAs were providing support for the teaching; in the other LEAs the impetus came from the schools themselves.
>
> (Hawkins 1996: 159)

The Pilot Scheme therefore represented a major departure for national primary education, and inevitably then secondary education. Access to the study of another language in the primary phase was being made available in the Pilot Scheme on an unprecedented scale.

## The Pilot Scheme: learning from the past

The undoubtedly extensive and comprehensive study conducted by Burstall and her team from the mid-1960s to the mid-1970s sought to 'discover whether it would be feasible and educationally desirable to extend the teaching of a foreign language to pupils who represented a wider range of age and ability than those to whom foreign languages had traditionally been taught' (Burstall et al. 1974: 11). The findings of this study remain central to our understanding of how we can plan for a successful integration of languages into the primary curriculum – and the pitfalls we must avoid.

The main aims of the study were cited as:

(i)  to investigate the long-term development of pupils' attitudes towards foreign language learning;

(ii)  to discover whether pupils' levels of achievements in French are significantly related to their attitudes towards foreign-language learning;

(iii)  to examine the effect of pupil variables (such as sex, age, socio-economic status, perception of parental encouragement, employment expectations, previous learning history, contact with France, etc.);

(iv)  to investigate whether teachers' attitudes and expectations significantly affect the attitudes and achievement of their pupils;

(v)  to investigate whether the early introduction of French has a significant effect on achievement in other areas of the primary school curriculum.

(Burstall et al. 1974: 13)

The findings were presented in comparative categories: the primary stage and the secondary stage, during which pupils were tracked beyond the primary school. Burstall found that attitudes towards modern language learning during both stages of the 'experiment' were 'positively and significantly related to their eventual level of achievement in that language. Throughout the period of the experiment, pupils' attitudes towards learning French and their level of proficiency in the language were in close association' (Burstall et al. 1974: 234). Girls generally outperformed boys throughout both stages of the Pilot Scheme, and those children with little expectation or aspiration of ever visiting France, or of securing employment in which French may be required as a practical skill, showed little motivation. The findings also consistently demonstrated a distinct correlation between achievement, attitude and social class, with those children from a less advantaged background performing less well than those from affluent backgrounds. Teachers' – including headteachers' – attitudes and expectations, were, not surprisingly, shown to have a major impact on the overall performance of pupils. In terms of general literacy and attainment, the findings were reported as follows:

> Taken as a whole, the results of the general attainment survey do not indicate that the introduction of French exerts any significant influence on achievement in other areas of the primary school curriculum. Variations in test performance were always accompanied by corresponding variations in the social composition of the groups concerned and there were no indications of a major trend in either a positive or a negative direction. The evidence does not lend support to the view that the introduction of a foreign language at the primary level must inevitably retard the acquisition of basic skills, nor does it

encourage the belief that teaching a foreign language to primary school children will necessarily stimulate the development of verbal skills in their mother tongue.

(Burstall et al. 1974: 42)

As Hoy (1977) points out, the research questions were formulated in the context of a 'profit and loss account':

> The researchers confined their conclusions to a 'profit and loss' account ... without trying to answer the question 'What are the conditions for success for primary French?' To have done so would have switched the conclusion from the retrospective to the forward-looking, from the depressing factual statement to the more inspiriting statement that future success was likely to result from the establishment of identifiable conditions.
>
> (quoted in Hawkins 1996: 162)

However, the researchers were unable to frame their conclusions in any context other than 'profit and loss'. Burstall is quite clear about this:

> The purpose of the NFER evaluation of the teaching of French in primary schools has been 'to provide proper evidence on which to base a decision for the future': 'The time for making a decision about whether a general advance should be made toward introducing French into all primary schools will come when the results of the formal evaluation are available, and plans can be made for the future, using the lessons that have been learnt' (Schools Council 1966). It had always been made clear that the Pilot Scheme had not been set up to establish whether or not it was possible to teach French in primary schools, but rather 'to find out the profit and loss of doing so' (Schools Council 1966).
>
> (Burstall et al. 1974: 241)

## Defining feasibility in the context of education policy

The notion of 'profit and loss' can be linked directly to the notion of 'feasible' in the original research question: 'even if Burstall (1974) had urged the expansion of primary French, the implementation of such advice would have been prevented by financial constraints and by the acute shortage of primary teachers who are competent in French' (Hoy 1977, quoted in Hawkins 1996). Indeed, 'resourcing' – specifically in terms of teacher knowledge and skills, training, equipment and materials remains one of the key issues in the current debate.

It is impossible to state to what extent the notions of 'feasible' and 'educationally desirable' were examined as separate issues, or indeed how these were precisely defined in the context of 'profit and loss'. Nor can any single reason for the rejection of the Pilot Scheme be identified as overriding. Researchers in the field have identified individual reasons for the rejection of the Pilot Scheme. Driscoll highlights, for example, the fact that 'no substantial gain in later attainment at the secondary school could be demon-strated' (Driscoll and Frost 1999: 1), while Hawkins (1996) asserts that the Pilot Scheme quickly 'ran out of control' organizationally *and* suffered from a massive shortage of suitably trained teachers, with no systematic, sustainable or time-appropriate training or development programme in place.

Given its rubric, the conclusions of the evaluation were hardly surprising. The Pilot Scheme revealed complex and wide-ranging implications for such an enormous programme of curriculum reform:

- investment
- appropriate training both in ITE and for in-service teachers
- ability and/or willingness of the class teacher to teach modern languages
- headteachers' and teachers' attitudes and assumptions
- literacy and oracy
- pupil motivation and attitudes
- curriculum design and development
- availability of suitable materials
- integration of languages into the primary curriculum
- transition from a primary programme of languages into secondary education, particularly given the lack of parity in provision
- primary pedagogy and language teaching methodology
- choice of language.

It is then at this stage of the evaluation that the Pilot Scheme – and so too the con-tinued provision of languages in the primary curriculum – would have profited from further investment to examine ways of removing barriers, resolving organizational and resourcing issues and, equally importantly, to build on and capitalize on those areas identified as successful. Instead, it was halted, and 40 years later, the key issues in the implementation of nationwide, *sustainable* programmes of primary languages are largely the same. McLachlan (2009b: 201) comments:

> Learning from the past, and thus identifying what needs to be in place to en-sure successful curriculum innovation, is integral to the longer-term successful outcomes of that innovation. In 1976, in a report written for the Council of Europe, Peter Hoy, former HMI, outlined a series of conditions for, and obsta-cles to, success for Early Teaching of Modern Languages (ETML) programmes. These included:
>
> - clarity of long-term educational aims and short-term objectives
> - an administrative framework to meet the following needs:
>   - ○ financial support;
>   - ○ teacher supply;
>   - ○ teacher-support services to provide advice, supervision, initial and in-service training resource centres and information services;
>   - ○ the need for continuity.

- co-ordination of modern language teaching with the rest of the primary curriculum.

(Hoy 1976: 3)

Where these conditions are not in place, Hoy argued, 'policy decisions may be based on unsound assumptions, and resources may be dissipated in unsuitable or counter-productive efforts' (1976: 5).

These conditions are as necessary today and can provide a framework at school, local and national level for establishing a successful model for primary languages teaching and learning.

## After the Pilot Scheme: moving towards a national strategy for languages

While small pockets of interest in the field of primary languages remained after the withdrawal of funding in 1975, it was not until the Nuffield Languages Inquiry (2000), that primary languages became once more the subject of educational debate. The Nuffield team was tasked with looking at 'the UK's capability in languages and to report on what we need to do as a nation to improve it' (2000: 4), and this heralded a rapid development in the field of primary languages. The first significant development arising from the Inquiry was the publication of the National Languages Strategy – *Languages for All: Languages for Life – A Strategy for England* (DfES 2002b). The Strategy addressed national concerns about the lack of both foreign language proficiency and cultural awareness and understanding in England, and professed its vision of language learning as 'a life-long skill – to be used in business and pleasure, to open up avenues of communication and exploration, and to promote, encourage and instill a broader cultural understanding' (2002b: 5). Its most radical proposal, however, was the commitment to provide access to a foreign language throughout KS2 by 2010.

However, the decline in numbers taking a foreign language to GCSE level has itself become a matter of concern since 2002 when the requirement to study a foreign language until the age of 16 was abolished, which has arguably rendered the success of the primary languages initiative even more important. Recent attempts to ensure schools meet targets for recruitment to MFL at post-14, new-style GCSE and 14–19 pathways have led to greater flexibility in language learning.

Of great import to the language teaching community, both at primary and secondary level, is the recent review of languages in the English curriculum conducted by Lord Dearing (*Languages Review*, Dearing and King 2007) which recommends that 'languages become part of the statutory curriculum at KS2 in primary schools, when it is next reviewed' (2007: 10). Thus, commitment by central government to the longer-term future of primary languages seems assured. It is also worth noting that subsequent DfES strategies, particularly *Excellence and Enjoyment: A Strategy for Primary Schools* (DfES 2003), *Every Child Matters* (DfES 2004a) and the *Five Year Strategy for Children and Learners* (DfES 2004b) are explicit in their aims to promote the ethos and implementation of the National Languages Strategy in primary schools, not only in terms of improving practical language skills, but also in terms of providing an enhanced curriculum and learning experience for all children. Similarly, the links between literacy – embodied in the National Literacy Strategy, which in 2003 became part of the Primary National Strategy – and foreign language learning, and how these may be developed and encouraged to facilitate higher attainment in both, are also being explored and promoted.

## Primary languages in England: the current picture and key challenges

There are a number of important studies that together provide a picture of current provision and progress towards ensuring the entitlement, see, for example, Powell et al. (2000), Martin (2000), Driscoll, Jones and Macrory (2004) and Muijs et al. (2005). Our own research indicates that successful long-term primary language teaching and learning will require an enormous commitment from central and local government, school leadership, and both primary and secondary practitioners. Learning conversations with Headteachers, teachers, teaching assistants, pupils and parents have enabled us to identify the following issues.

### Status and priority of primary languages

- Primary languages remain somewhat of a movable feast in the primary curriculum, often being moved or cancelled altogether for extra-curricular or other activities. This again compromises learning, and reinforces the perception of languages as 'not a serious subject'.
- Primary languages remain fairly low on schools' priorities, mostly due to perceived pressure to perform well in national testing. Some schools report that the recent promotion of sports, music and drama initiatives seems to have overtaken existing primary languages initiatives.

### Timetabling language teaching and learning

- Allocating discrete curriculum time for languages provision remains largely problematic for a variety of reasons, but where frequent and regular lessons are not provided, learning is compromised.
- The National Languages Strategy recommends one hour a week of language teaching and learning, and this does not have to be a single block of discrete teaching. Many schools allocate as little as 20 minutes to languages, which impacts severely upon pupils' ability to embed language. Thus, progression in learning is inevitably slow or even indiscernible.
- The enormous diversity in time allocated to primary languages in schools causes problems in planning for learning KS3 in terms of pupils' prior knowledge.

## Teaching and learning

- There is little awareness of what may constitute 'high quality teaching and learning' in the context of early language teaching and learning.
- Many teachers have not consulted the KS2 Framework for languages, and are not applying it in their short-term or longer-term planning. Thus schools continue to offer very diverse programmes of language teaching and learning as they are not operating within a single framework of practice.

## Enhancing learning across the curriculum and cross-curricular approaches to language teaching and learning

- There is as yet little evidence to suggest a systematic approach to linking language learning with literacy, or other areas of the curriculum.
- Many teachers remain unclear about how primary languages can support learning across the curriculum.

## Assessment

- Assessment policies are largely underdeveloped in schools, and this renders capturing attainment data on a national scale problematic.
- Embedding Assessment for Learning (AfL) in primary languages teaching and learning is not current practice in many schools, even though AfL approaches are used widely in other areas of the curriculum.
- Many teachers are opposed to the notion of assessing attainment in primary languages for a variety of reasons, including additional workload, lack of understanding of what reasonable 'attainment' is and their ability to capture it.
- Many also feel that languages are essentially a 'fun' subject, and should remain *de facto* free of assessment.

## Transition: progression and continuity in learning

- Extreme diversity of provision within primary schools, and lack of coordinated planning with secondary schools, threaten both continuity and progression, and inevitably impact upon pupil learning outcomes.
- Schools are aware of the importance of planning for languages in conjunction with their secondary colleagues. However, they cite a number of barriers to effective planning, including time and a perceived unwillingness on the part of secondary schools to adapt existing KS3 Schemes of Work (SoW).
- Some schools are unaware of the role of the Specialist Language College (SLC) in the provision of specialist support staff, training, funding or teaching resources.

## Teacher attitudes to primary languages

- Some teachers remain unconvinced of the potential for enhancing literacy or oracy skills through primary languages, and view it as an unnecessary distraction from core subjects.
- Teachers' lack of confidence, or unwillingness to teach primary languages, are often directly related to their perceived or actual lack of subject knowledge.
- While many teachers remain unaware of the intended goals of the National Languages Strategy, they nonetheless largely support the inclusion of languages in the primary curriculum, though overwhelmingly because they perceive it as a 'fun' break from 'real learning'.

## Learning in international contexts

- Schools are keen to 'twin' with schools in other countries, particularly via e-twinning and videoconferencing (VC). They cite lack of support in these initiatives, particularly in terms of funding, as key barriers to developing partnerships with other countries.

## Building capacity and training

- Current capacity remains negligible – given that ensuring a sustainable supply of appropriately qualified and trained teachers is central to the eventual success of the strategy, there are clear implications for both CPD and ITE. Training programmes do not necessarily address a range of teacher competences, such as understanding the role of both the subject leader and the subject mentor, developing subject knowledge, acquiring skills in age-appropriate language teaching methodology, understanding the scope of primary languages.

## Sustainability

- Schools are not yet in a position to offer sustainable programmes of primary languages programmes without recourse to outside specialists, who may be sourced either from commercial companies, local SLCs, local secondary schools or other contacts. Thus, in many schools, current provision remains at risk.
- Where a single teacher is responsible for provision of primary languages across the whole school, this can lead to tension among staff. There is also concern that teachers will become deskilled in other areas of the curriculum if

they are to continue to assume responsibility for whole-school provision. Inevitably, this means that where teachers are not required to deliver primary languages, there is no impetus for them to develop their skills to enable them to do so.

## Leadership

- The role of the primary languages subject leader is increasingly common in schools, and is clearly necessary to maintain some form of consistency, though the functions of the role differs dramatically from school to school.
- Many schools do not yet have any formal policy for the inclusion of primary languages into the curriculum. Where primary languages are not part of the School Improvement Plan, it is likely that the status and priority of languages are very low. Where there is a structured primary languages policy in line with the whole-school plan, languages programmes are likely to be more successfully embedded.
- Where the Headteacher has a positive attitude towards primary languages, this is likely to enhance the profile of the subject in the school community.

## Funding streams

- Availability of, and funding for, appropriate materials and resources, are perceived by schools as very important, and would appear to be lacking on a coordinated scale. Furthermore, schools remain largely unaware of what funding streams are available, and how to access them.

---

## Activity

Reflect on the background to the development of primary languages in England, paying particular attention to the reasons why the 'French from Eight' scheme was unsuccessful, and what we as a teaching community might learn from this. Relate these to the points identified in the section. 'Primary languages in England: the current picture and key challenges' on pp. 12–5, and with reference to your preliminary observations in school, discuss as a group reasonable ways of promoting effective and sustainable programmes of primary languages teaching and learning.

## Conclusion

We are now in a strong position to learn from the past and build on it to promote effective and sustainable practice, and to ensure that primary languages will become an embedded and valued part of an enriched primary curriculum. Facilitating structured and longer-term planning, defining reasonable and appropriate objectives, and equipping our new and existing primary practitioners with the knowledge, skills and resources will play a pivotal role in achieving that goal.

# 2 Becoming a primary languages practitioner

This chapter discusses:

- principles for effective primary practice
- the professional profile of the primary languages practitioner
- teacher competences in primary languages
- the role and scope of subject knowledge in primary languages practice, with reference to the standards for QTS
- cultural awareness and intercultural understanding in the context of primary languages
- understanding child language development and its implications for classroom practice
- assessing and improving language skills
- professional learning in a community of practice, and the need to engage as a lifelong learner.

## Teaching and learning in the primary languages classroom

The successful primary languages teacher is first and foremost an effective *primary practitioner*. Thus, as you develop core and increasingly advanced skills and competences in primary teaching and learning, these will *de facto* support and enhance your development as a primary languages practitioner. As we will discuss in further detail in Chapter 3, there are fundamental principles for teaching and learning which apply across the curriculum. *Curriculum Guidance for the Foundation Stage* (QCA 2000) identifies a set of principles for early years education including:

- There should be opportunities for children to engage in activities planned by adults and also those that they plan or initiate themselves.
- Well-planned, purposeful activity and appropriate intervention by practitioners will engage children in the learning process.
- For children to have rich and stimulating experiences, the learning environment should be well planned and well organized.

These principles contribute equally meaningfully to planning across KS2, and are complemented by a set of principles for learning and teaching enshrined in *Excellence and Enjoyment: Learning and Teaching in the Primary Years* (DfES 2004c) (see Box 2.1).

# Box 2.1  Principles for learning and teaching

*Set high expectations and give every learner confidence they can succeed*
This includes:

- demonstrating a commitment to every learner's success, making them feel included, valued and secure;
- raising learners' aspirations and the effort they put into learning, engaging, where appropriate, the active support of parents or carers.

*Establish what learners already know and build on it*
This includes:

- setting clear and appropriate learning goals, explaining them, and making every learning experience count;
- creating secure foundations for subsequent learning.

*Structure and pace the learning experience to make it challenging and enjoyable*
This includes:

- using teaching methods that reflect the material to be learned, matching the maturity of the learners and their learning preferences, and involving high levels of time on task;
- making creative use of the range of learning opportunities available, within and beyond the classroom, including ICT.

*Inspire learning through passion for the subject*
This includes:

- bringing the subject alive;
- making it relevant to learners' wider goals and concerns.

*Make individuals active partners in their learning*
This includes:

- building respectful teacher–learner relationships that take learners' views and experience fully into account, as well as data on their performance;
- using assessment for learning to help learners assess their work, reflect on how they learn, and inform subsequent planning and practice.

*Develop learning skills*
This includes:

- developing the ability to think systematically, manage information, learn from others and help others learn;
- developing confidence, self-discipline and an understanding of the learning process.

Taken from: www.standards.dfes.gov.uk/seu/coreprinciples1/core-principles.doc. Developed from *Excellence and Enjoyment: Learning and Teaching in the Primary Years* (DfES 2004c: 15).

Additionally, understanding how children learn, and equally importantly, how we can help them to develop as learners, is a key skill in the primary practitioner's repertoire. *Excellence and Enjoyment* offers the following guidance:

> Learning can and does happen in a range of ways and in a variety of contexts. Learning is not always predictable – sometimes we learn in unexpected ways or learn things we did not set out to learn. Teachers ... can do much to help children to develop as learners. To do this, they carefully design the curriculum, taking into account:
>
> - the content it offers
> - how it is experienced, taught and assessed
> - how it is adapted and amended to engage all children and personalized to meet their needs and abilities.
>
> (DfES 2004c: 6)

Thus, if we are to achieve a truly integrated and successful outcome for primary languages, teachers must apply the same practice to their languages programmes as they do to the rest of the curriculum.

## The professional profile of the primary languages practitioner

The question of who is best placed to teach primary languages has long been recognized as an issue of some complexity. In 1999, Sharpe summarized the issue thus:

> ultimately there are only two possible options for staffing primary modern language teaching: either the pupils are taught by a specialist of some kind or they are taught by the generalist primary class teacher who is responsible for delivering all or most of the curriculum.
>
> (in Driscoll and Frost 1999: 165)

There are, however, a number of definitions of 'specialist' ranging from trained secondary language teachers who may have little or no knowledge or understanding of either the primary curriculum, or theories underpinning early learning, to native speakers who may not have either that, or any formal teacher training. The marriage of a degree of subject knowledge, i.e. a baseline competence in a particular language, *and* expertise in primary pedagogy is one which is sensibly beginning to emerge as a model of good practice. Indeed, as early as 1997, some five years before the publication of the National Languages Strategy, the Association for Language Learning (ALL) highlighted the need for a clear and 'long-term' plan to introduce languages into ITE in the primary sector (ALL 1997). The advent of primary languages specialism programmes in 2001, the *Initial Teacher Training Primary Languages Project,* a shared initiative involving the Teacher Training Agency (TTA, now TDA) and partner institutions in Europe (France, Germany, Spain), with additional support from the Centre for Information on Language Teaching and Research (CILT, now the National Centre for Languages), created a new model of primary languages specialist – a primary practitioner with a specialist expertise in language teaching and learning, thus creating specialists within the primary teaching community it-self.

## Teacher competences in primary languages

Driscoll, Jones and Macrory have recently confronted the issue of teacher compe-tence in the context of primary languages in England. They define competence as concerned with the 'knowledge, skills and ability of the teacher' (2004: 3). This is par-ticularly pertinent in the field of primary languages. It is recognized that there is a widespread shortage of trained Primary Languages specialists and while this is gradu-ally being addressed, the wording of the primary languages entitlement is open to a number of interpretations. Schools may employ a 'wide range of individuals' to de-liver the entitlement, such as 'native speakers and those with strong language skills within our community and within business' (DfES 2002b). As a pool to *draw on* for additional support, this is a potentially sound strategy. However, as a model for *de-livery*, we would argue that this serves to undermine the notion of teacher compe-tence and expertise. The deployment of secondary teachers in primary schools may address the issue of subject knowledge and subject-specific pedagogy, in the short term, but singularly fails to acknowledge the importance of expertise in primary ped-agogy. Equally unsatisfactory as a long-term solution is the sole deployment of pri-mary class teachers lacking in expertise in both subject knowledge and subject-specific pedagogy.

In answer to the research question 'What teacher competences are required to teach foreign languages effectively in the later primary phase?', the team concluded, not surprisingly, that teacher knowledge was central to effective teaching. They defined teacher knowledge in the context of primary languages as follows:

- the subject
  - the foreign language content (e.g. verbs and nouns)
  - the skills to use the target language in clearly defined areas for commu-nication
  - the target culture
- subject-specific teaching methods
- age-specific teaching methods
- resources
- primary curriculum
- children as individuals
- children's learning needs.

This definition provides the primary languages community with an invaluable rubric for the professional development of effective primary languages practitioners.

# Defining subject knowledge in primary languages

Our research, resonating with findings from a number of studies, reveals that lack of confidence in subject knowledge, and the application of subject knowledge in the classroom, coupled with a 'fear of the unknown', are key barriers to the successful development of primary languages programmes among both teachers and trainees. One teacher told us:

> Asking me to teach a foreign language is like asking me to fix a leaking radiator. I wouldn't know where to start, I don't know how it works, and I don't know how to go about finding the problem and fixing it, and I'm not sure I want to really, some of my kids can't even speak English properly.

A large number of trainees on non-specialist pathways have expressed similar concerns. In terms of policy, the review of teacher competence in the field of primary languages (Driscoll, Jones and Macrory 2004: 6) highlight the needs for the provision of

> varied teacher training programmes and sustained professional development opportunities for primary school teachers to enable them to develop and maintain their subject knowledge, especially in terms of language proficiency and cultural knowledge, as well as language-specific teaching strategies for primary age learners.

Ofsted (2008) defines strong subject knowledge in primary languages as:

- quality of main teaching language;
- knowing how to use the target language with pupils;
- knowledge and understanding of:
    - links with English and literacy
    - links with other languages (including their pupils' languages)
    - cross-curricular linking generally
    - intercultural awareness
    - the KS2 Framework for languages, the Key Stage 3 Framework
    - the Qualifications and Curriculum Authority schemes of work
    - the Languages Ladder
    - the international dimension.

and reported that:

> A strength of trainees' subject knowledge was their understanding of how languages can be successfully integrated into the primary curriculum. They applied their knowledge of another language and culture to their growing understanding of the primary curriculum very well and often sought creative opportunities to develop new links for pupils and develop their thinking. This resulted in pupils' enjoyment when they spotted connections between different areas of the curriculum ... The best trainees also applied very effectively

the intercultural understanding they had gained from their placement abroad. Trainees also knew how to adapt teaching techniques, strategies and resources from their generic primary training to the languages classroom. For example, the best trainees applied generic principles of assessment – often an underdeveloped area of primary languages teaching – to their foreign language work.

(2008: 11)

Having a secure knowledge of a subject is in itself insufficient to ensure effective teaching and learning of that subject. It is essential that primary languages teachers are absolutely clear about what language or cultural input they are teaching, why they are teaching it, in what sequence they are teaching it, how this relates to what pupils' language learning in particular, and wider learning in general, and the use pupils can make of that learning. *Teacher language*, that is, the language a teacher uses to explain and demonstrate concepts and notions, and to provide opportunities for learners to engage with those concepts and notions, is absolutely central to ensuring that good teaching – and sound learning – takes place. Pachler and Field (2001: 20) note this point also, stating:

> Subject knowledge can be seen as a high level of proficiency in, and good structural knowledge, as well as the ability to make effective use of the TL, wide-ranging awareness of the culture(s) of the countries where the TL is spoken, some knowledge of the linguistic theories underpinning the language learning/acquisition process as well as a familiarity with the respective statutory framework and related document.

Of course, a primary general practitioner, even one who has completed a Primary Languages Specialism, cannot be expected to possess the same depth of subject knowledge as a secondary languages specialist, but we would argue that the broader sense of this definition of subject knowledge is relevant to primary languages practice. Pachler and Field (2001) adapt Shulman's seven categories of teacher knowledge to identify key subject knowledge and subject application competences in the language teacher's repertoire. Here we list the categories, with specific reference to the standards for QTS and apply them to the primary languages practitioner:

1. *Content knowledge* – the core content, both linguistic and cultural, that is to be taught, and the need for teachers to engage in iterative professional learning to ensure this is up-to-date and relevant; an understanding of how the appropriate use of ICT can enhance both teaching and learning (Q7, Q8, Q14, Q17, Q23).

2. *General pedagogical knowledge* – the underpinning principles of teaching and learning, classroom management and the development of the child; an ineffective primary practitioner will by definition be an ineffective primary languages practitioner (Q10, Q11, Q12, Q18, Q22, Q23, Q27, Q28, Q31).

3. *Curriculum knowledge* – an understanding of the scope of both the KS2 Framework for Languages and the QCA Schemes of Work; the range of language appropriate to KS2 and the primary curriculum as a whole in order to

ensure an integrated and cross-curricular approach to language teaching and learning (*Q14, Q15, Q22, Q23*).

4   *Pedagogical/content knowledge* – an ability to deconstruct language in order to represent it in appropriate ways to ensure pupil understanding and learning; the ability to demonstrate and model good and *relevant* linguistic models (*Q14, Q15, Q22, Q23*).

5   *Knowledge of learners and their characteristics* – awareness and understanding of pupils' personalities, prior learning and preferred learning styles; awareness and understanding of pupils' attainment across the curriculum, with particular reference to their specific learning targets – this will enable the primary languages practitioners to design opportunities for learning which will support the achievement of those targets (*Q1, Q4, Q10, Q13, Q18, Q19, Q24, Q28, Q29*).

6   *Knowledge of educational contexts* – ensuring that the teaching and learning of modern languages complements the whole-school vision for learning; understanding the home and wider social environment within which individual pupils operate, with particular emphasis on languages other than English spoken in out-of-school contexts (*Q3b, Q6, Q13, Q19, Q21*).

7   *Knowledge of educational ends, purposes and values, and philosophical and historical background* – knowledge and understanding of the developments in primary languages teaching, the key aims and objectives of primary languages both at national and local level (*Q3b, Q14, Q15*).

## Cultural awareness and competence

It is impossible to learn a language and to learn to teach a language without engaging with its culture, and in fact, many teachers will be motivated by their love of the culture and the associated experiences they have enjoyed. Culture is sometimes defined in terms of a content and Curtain and Pesola's (1994) suggested cultural content for primary children based on representations of other cultures in environments familiar to the children is a useful starting point. The categories they propose are cultural symbols such as flags and national flowers, products such as stories and currency and practices such as greetings, food and drink and festivals. Curtain and Pesola's categories are in evidence as the cultural linchpin of most primary approaches to cultural learning and feature prominently in most course material. These thus form the knowledge baseline with which teachers need to be familiar.

Doyé (1999) adopts a step-by-step approach to developing young children's cultural competence involving:

- the selection of learner-appropriate contents;
- relativizing the opposition – them and us;
- taking perspectives and decentring;
- modifying stereotypes;

- unlearning prejudice;
- preventing discrimination;
- acquiring tolerance.

These process-focused steps indicate a move from knowledge about customs and arti-facts and cultural awareness towards intercultural understanding that involves personal engagement, reflection and an understanding that culture is dynamic and contested. Such an approach requires learners, be they pupils or teachers, to reflect critically on their own culture as well as the target culture to create what Kramsch (1993) calls 'a sphere of interculturality' and intercultural understanding. Doyé's steps stand good as a cultural learning agenda for trainees during the period abroad (see Chapter 10) and in the necessary lifelong engagement with the target culture alongside continuous up-dating about 'cultural symbols, products and practices'. Kirsch emphasizes that as a language teacher, you aid the development of intercultural competence when 'your teaching goes beyond the knowledge of, for example, a culture's artefacts and ways of life, and includes a focus on attitudes and skills' (2008: 169).

---

## Activity

In small groups, conduct an audit of your current skills and competences with specific reference to both the areas outlined by Ofsted, and the seven key subject knowledge and subject application competences. Feed back to the whole group, outlining targets for professional development, taking suggestions from your fellow students.

---

### Assessing and improving language skills

While the scope of 'subject knowledge' encompasses more than proficiency in the target language, clearly, teachers must *de facto* have a certain competence in the subject itself, before they can begin to understand the methodologies and strategies for teaching it. Achieving a sufficient competence in the target language is a major challenge to trainees, teachers and training providers, with arguably much of the onus falling on practitioners to assume responsibility for improving their own language skills to ensure a baseline level of linguistic competence. As McLachlan (2009b: 198) notes:

> Another factor that will begin to impact upon primary languages training very soon is the increasing number of trainees who, because of the KS4 opt-out, will themselves not have studied a language beyond Year 9. The challenge for trainers is then twofold, and mirrors that of the primary schools themselves: how to fit language teaching methodology for young learners into an already intensive training programme, and how to equip beginning teachers with even a baseline subject knowledge which will enable them to teach it. This concern was raised by [the] Deputy Head ...: 'To me, at the moment, we seem to be teaching teachers to teach a language who don't have a background with the

language, and can't call on a vocabulary and grammatical knowledge.' Thus we are creating a situation where our future teachers, with little or no competence in a modern language themselves, will be called upon to contribute to a 'renaissance' in language learning, which they will clearly not be able to do in any meaningful way. A possible – if not the only – solution, already recommended by Hawkins in 1996, is to introduce an entry requirement of a minimum GCSE in one European language for all those wishing to train as primary teachers, and I would argue, to supplement that with a skills test prior to admission on a training programme, in a similar vein to English, Maths and ICT. A primary teaching community without secure subject knowledge in other areas of the curriculum would be unacceptable, so what does it say about the priority and status of primary languages when it appears that in this curriculum area it *is* acceptable?

Specialism programmes may require degree-level competence, though many specify a minimum of a strong A-Level or equivalent. Before you can improve existing skills, you need to have an understanding of what those skills are. The TDA recommends a minimum of B1 on the *Common European Framework of Reference* (CEF), which is roughly equivalent to the English A-Level. For detailed information, refer to: http://www.coe.int/T/DG4/Linguistic/CADRE_EN.asp.

It can be challenging to improve your language skills alone, and both trainees and teachers often find that attending a night school course is unrealistic in terms of workload and time available. During campus-based training, you will find it useful to meet as a group on a regular basis, with specific language learning tasks and target-setting. Knowledge of both core and extension language appropriate to KS2 is essential, and you should consult the QCA KS2 Schemes of Work and ensure you have a mastery of this content. It is also important to understand the range and scope of the KS3 Schemes of Work, not only to assist longer-term planning and transition issues, but also to challenge more able linguists, or G&T pupils, in your primary classroom. You will find these at:

> French:
> http://www.standards.dfes.gov.uk/schemes2/secondary_mff/?view=get

> German:
> http://www.standards.dfes.gov.uk/schemes2/secondary_mfg/?view=get

> Spanish:
> http://www.standards.dfes.gov.uk/schemes2/secondary_mfs/?view=get

## Activity
### A preliminary language learning session on a primary languages specialism

* Write approximately 400 words on a topic which interests you in your target language. Read around the topic first via target language websites or other sources.

- As a whole group, spend about 15 minutes reading two to three texts written by your colleagues.
- As you read, pick out the key points of information, and note them in writing in the target language (TL).
- Try to identify what you consider to be errors.
- After reading the texts, ask each other questions in the TL based on information in the text, trying to gather more information.
- Present your summary of the text in key points in the TL to the whole group.
- As a whole group, identify what you consider to be the most commonly occurring errors and see if you can correct them together.
- Choose a text other than your own and read it out loud to the rest of the group, with particular focus on your pronunciation and delivery – think about what makes an audience want to listen to a speaker and try to emulate those characteristics as you read.
- Decide as a group what the next language learning activity should be.

**Discussion points**

- Current personal subject knowledge skills – how do you assess them? Plans for developing them over the coming months? Remember to be realistic about the amount of time you can reasonably devote to developing your language skills.
- List what you have identified as the most commonly occurring errors, and discuss ways these can be addressed.
- Brainstorm what makes a 'good' speaker – what are the implications for how you might speak in front of a class?

## Understanding child language development, and its implications for classroom practice

As a child enters primary education, what stage of linguistic development has he or she reached, and how can this inform our practice as primary languages teachers? Cameron (2001: 12) points out that the acquisition of a child's first language is still very much in development at that age, with formal literacy skills, which we categorize as reading and writing, in the early stages of development. Lightbown and Spada (1999: 2) highlight this too, and make the important point that:

> Children's ability to understand language and to use it to express themselves develops rapidly in the pre-school years. *Metalinguistic awareness* – the ability to treat language as an object, separate from the meaning it conveys – develops more slowly. A dramatic development in metalinguistics awareness occurs when children begin to learn to read. Although metalinguistic awareness

begins to develop well before this time, seeing words represented by letters on a page leads children to a new level of awareness of language.

For us, this is not an argument against the introduction of structured input on reading and writing in a second language, rather, it is a clear rationale for doing so – as children acquire the generic skills that enable them to access, and to enjoy, reading and writing, we believe that practitioners can harness that phase of development, and apply the same teaching strategies in the primary languages classroom.

In terms of speaking skills, or 'discourse skills' (Cameron 2001), practitioners need to be aware that these too are in a continuous phase of development in the first language, and that the exposure a child has to different kinds of language in out-of-school environments impacts significantly upon their linguistic development: 'a connection has been found between children's early experiences with language use in their families, and their language development in various domains' (2001: 12). Thus, as in every other curriculum area, teachers need to take into account that some children are more advanced, or able, linguists than others, and bring with them differently developed skills and learning abilities in their first language. Pinter (2006) discusses the role of input and interaction in a child's first experiences of language. She cites a 1972 study looking at how mothers interact verbally with their babies which showed that:

> Mothers' speech to their babies was slower and more repetitive than their normal speech to adults. They used various simplifications and modifications in their speech and these were shown to be very helpful in making the input comprehensible to children. Such simplified talk contains a lot of repetition, a slower rate of speech, exaggerated intonation patterns . . . carers typically talk about topic areas immediately relevant to the child such as the family, home environment, toys, animals, body parts, and food.
>
> (2006: 19)

## Teachers talking

A Year 4 Primary German teacher talks about how he approached the first term of German:

> For me, the challenge was to ensure they could learn gradually, and use the language they were learning in a progressive way. So I knew I was going to have to move from individual words, then to simple sentences, then to more complex structures, but that it would take time. I wanted very much to acknowledge that these were Year 4 children, aged 7 and 8, and whilst their English is still developing, the strategies they use to develop their English skills are not structured around baby-talk, and I wanted to give them an appropriate intellectual challenge, without expecting them to master connectives and conjunctions that send verbs to the end of sentences! I found

that repetitive activities, and lots of repetition in general, did work well, so long as I kept it short and sweet, and went on to something else before boredom set in. I'd be bored too if someone kept saying 'It is a dog, it is a dog, is it a dog?' over and over again, without giving me something to actually do with the structures and words I'm learning. What we absolutely have to avoid is expecting them to produce something in German that they have not yet fully grasped in English, and we have to remember that their exposure to German, with the best will in the world, remains very limited, so their progress will be slower, it won't keep pace with English. So I accepted one- or two-word utterances and answers for a long time – I don't agree with the 'give me a full sentence' school of thought, adults don't always answer in full sentences in their first language. I let them make mistakes, and we unpick them together – but not always – I let a lot go when we're speaking, why interrupt the flow constantly? It can really demotivate children, and it's good that they experiment, they do that in their first language, and make lots of errors in that too. It's all part of the process. So long as children are engaging with the language, and seeing ways of expressing themselves in an increasingly sophisticated way, and trying things out, that's fine by me.

The primary languages community of practice is strengthened by a knowledge of theoretical considerations deriving from extensive research over the years that has furnished important theories of learning and language learning. These theories show that children learn through an active process of sense-making based on their experiences, with the potential in the classroom for varied and extended opportunities for learning. Language in particular provides the child with a tool to aid cognitive development. The child is also a social being and learns through engagement with other children and with adults who mediate the world and make it accessible. Research has shown a facility in young children for foreign language learning (regardless of whether any gains are sustained), based on, for example, their skill for mimicry, enjoyment of wordplay and constructivist approach to learning. Partridge (1994), for example, argues that metalinguistic awareness plays an important role in language development and, consequently, has implications for foreign language learning. Certainly, making explicit links between English and the target language is one of the key objectives of the framework, outlined in the strand of KAL (knowledge about language), providing a rich basis for engaging with the functions of language by comparing both similarities and differences.

The foreign language classroom (notwithstanding Taeschner's research (1991) that signalled a need for teachers to be sensitive to the difficulties young children may experience during a parallel process of acquiring the mother tongue and learning a foreign language), can provide a learning environment that supports the child's language, cognitive and social development as well as cultural knowledge and intercultural understanding through the development of children's curiosity, tolerance and appreciation towards other cultures. The development of such skills and knowledge is a *sine qua non* of a balanced primary learning curriculum and of the European citizens of tomorrow.

It can be seen that the subject knowledge required of an effective primary languages teacher draws on many disciplines and experiences. The effective primary languages teacher has subject knowledge rich in child development, language development, and both linguistic and cultural knowledge which all mesh together to create an effective pedagogy for a successful language learning classroom community. It is useful for you to observe and analyse different teaching approaches in order to establish what constitutes *effective* practice.

# Lifelong learning

Subject knowledge maintenance is a lifelong learning task. Linguistic knowledge can quickly get rusty if one does not maintain contact with the target language as new vocabulary and turns of phrase enter mainstream use on an almost daily basis. Similarly it is important not to be left in a cultural time warp and to keep up to date with cultural knowledge and to develop further intercultural competence. The responsibility for keeping up to date is on the individual teacher who needs to maintain an awareness of the range of possibilities, many of them funded for language teachers. First ports of call should be the LA Adviser, The National Centre for Languages (CILT) and the Embassies who often provide subsidized study visits. After that, there are a great many commercial courses available to be considered as well as private arrangements to be made. Although teachers of all subjects have a responsibility to keep their subject knowledge updated, for language teachers there is no substitute for spending time in the country, an added bonus for this group of specialists. Language teachers invariably want to pass on their passion for the language and the country to their pupils and organizing visits for pupils is one powerful way to do this. It is very valuable experience to be involved in the planning of such a trip and to accompany the children if possible.

## Collaborative professional learning: the primary languages community

Networking with other practitioners, and operating within a wider community of practice, are essential to the professional development of teachers. Within your own region, you can make contact with other primary schools and liaise with your LA Primary Languages Adviser, in order to share good practice and develop new ways of working. Becoming part of an online community broadens your opportunities for professional learning, allowing you to communicate with colleagues nationally, and a good starting point is the website developed by CILT, dedicated to the promotion of primary languages practice: http://www.primarylanguages.org.uk/. The site aims to provide practitioners with an overview of issues in primary languages, and offers materials, resources, interviews, a comprehensive media library, links to key related websites and other relevant information such as training and language courses. The site complements the NACELL (National Advisory Centre for Early Language Learning) website www.nacell.org.uk. Via the NACELL website you can join a number of valuable online communities and discussion lists, such as the ELL Forum (Early Language Learning) or the ITTMFL Forum (Initial Teacher Training in Modern Foreign Languages). You can also subscribe to the CILT *Primary Languages Direct E-zine*.

## Conclusion

The key to effective primary languages practice lies in both the acquisition of skills in effective primary practice as a whole, and in a certain level of skill in, and knowledge of, the language and the cultures of the people who speak it. Subject knowledge, which encompasses knowledge of the range of the subject, its application in a classroom setting, and pedagogic understanding, and how these interrelate, are essential core competences which begin to develop during the initial training year, and continue to evolve throughout the practitioner's career.

# 3 Effective planning in primary languages

This chapter discusses how to:

- understand the role, structure and content of the KS2 Framework for Languages and the QCA Schemes of Work, and how these contribute to cross-curricular learning
- use the framework to plan for progression in learning across KS2
- ensure progression in language learning: using the Attainment Targets
- begin to adopt a cross-curricular approach to language teaching and learning
- identify features of best practice in planning primary languages lessons
- design an effective lesson plan template for primary languages
- introduce short-, medium- and longer-term planning into primary languages programmes
- work successfully with a teaching or foreign language assistant.

## Understanding the role of the KS2 Framework for Languages

The rationale for the development of the KS2 Framework for Languages is to firmly embed the provision of languages programmes into the ethos of the national primary curriculum, and to reflect the aims and intentions of *Every Child Matters: Change for Children* (DfES 2004a) and *Excellence and Enjoyment: A Strategy for Primary Schools* (DfES 2003). As we saw in Chapter 1, the broader rationale for primary education is to promote creativity, create independent learners, and to broaden horizons. It is important to note that the Framework is not a *national curriculum* for languages at KS2, but rather a 'core document, offering a practical reference tool for planning, teaching and monitoring the learning process ... designed to support primary school teachers in building their own courses' (DfES 2005: 3). Trainees and primary practitioners may initially feel overwhelmed by the sheer size of the framework, and thus it is important to take time to familiarize yourself with it gradually. Although the application of the Framework itself is not statutory, it remains a key reference text for primary languages. In terms of both the new professional standards for teachers, for example, Q15, 'Know and understand the relevant statutory and non-statutory curricula and frameworks, including those provided through the National Strategies, for their subjects/curriculum areas, and other relevant initiatives applicable to the age and ability range for which they are trained' (TDA 2007: 9), and to ensure consistency of provision at a national level, it is important for practitioners to begin to work within it.

## Structure and content of the Framework

The Framework itself covers the range of KS2, Years 3–6. The clearly structured and progressive set of teaching and learning objectives across KS2 is particularly useful for beginning primary languages practitioners, as it offers an overview of how learning can take place, and progress successfully. It should be noted that it is based upon a structured model of language learning which begins at Year 3, and works across KS2 up to the end of Year 6. However, it is equally appropriate to adapt the Framework to suit particular contexts, to 'support primary school teachers to build their own courses'. Thus, if a Year 6 group is being introduced to a new language, teachers may choose to follow a blend of content from Years 3–6, adapting the delivery of the learning objectives to ensure an appropriate level of challenge for older learners.

The Framework is underpinned by five key inter-related strands – three 'core' strands and two 'cross-cutting' strands. They have clear links to both the Primary National Curriculum, and the 12 learning strands of the Primary Framework for Literacy (see Chapter 1).

The core strands are:

- Oracy: listening, speaking, spoken interaction (O);
- Literacy: reading and writing (L);
- Intercultural understanding (IU): develop greater understanding of their own lives, look at things from other perspectives, insight into people, culture and traditions of other countries.

The 'cross-cutting' strands are:

- Knowledge about language (KAL): develop insights into the nature of language and its social and cultural value, develop understanding of how language works;
- Language learning strategies (LLS): develop strategies applicable to the learning of any language, including their own, develop awareness of their own preferred learning strategies.

The Framework comprises three key sections, each with a particular range of focus:

*Part 1: (P1-90)*

- clear outline of expectations and outcomes per year group (e.g. P18) with ideas for classroom practice;
- a year-by-year guide to teaching and learning objectives (e.g. P56): a learning objective can be identified as follows: O3.1; note that each core strand is noted by its first letter;
- planning for progression: an overview of each strand per year group (e.g. P67);

- useful year-group colour-coding: Year 3 is red, Year 4 is orange, Year 5 is green, Year 6 is lilac.

*Part 2: (P1-71)*

- organizational and institutional issues;
- tips for getting the most out of the Framework;
- advice on implementing languages into the primary curriculum;
- advice on how to get started, then moving on;
- advice for secondary school languages staff, which can provide a valuable template for discussions between primary and secondary practitioners when preparing for transition.

*Part 3: (P1-136)*

- emphasis on embedding the Framework into planning;
- a comprehensive bank of teaching activities per year group;
- guidance on cross-curricular approaches;
- examples of medium-term and longer-term planning;
- inclusion, incorporating Every Child Matters, SEN, support strategies for all abilities, English as an Additional Language (EAL)
- further guidance on managing transition and ensuring continuity in learning;
- assessment, and recording progress;
- working with mixed year groups.

---

## Box 3.1 Understanding the language and core content of the Framework

The language of the Framework objectives is specific to the core strands, the particular year group, and the objective 'number'. There are generally either three or four individual objectives per strand, per year group:

**O3.1** *Listen and respond to simple rhymes, stories and songs* refers to **Oracy Year 3, Objective 1**.
**L4.2** *Follow a short familiar text, listening and reading at the same time* refers to **Literacy Year 4, Objective 2**.
**IU5.3** *Compare symbols, objects or products which represent their own culture with those of another country* refers to **Intercultural Understanding, Year 5, Objective 3**.

The cross-cutting strands of *knowledge about language* (KAL) and *language learning strategies* (LLS) do not have specific objectives, but clear guidance is given on activities which directly promote them. Look at this extract from Year 6 at a glance:

**O6.1** *Understand the main points in a spoken story, song or passage*
**L6.4** *Write sentences on a range of topics using a model*
**IU6.3** *Present information about an aspect of culture*

---

**Knowledge about language (KAL)**

- recognize patterns in the foreign language;
- notice and match agreements;
- use knowledge of words, text and structure to build simple spoken and written passages.

**Language learning strategies (LLS)**

- plan and prepare – analyse what needs to be done in order to carry out a task;
- use language known in one context or topic in another context or topic;
- use context and previous knowledge to help understanding and reading skills.

(Part 1, Page 57)

## The QCA Schemes of Work

The QCA Schemes of Work provide an invaluable resource for teachers, and have been developed with clear reference to both the KS2 Framework for Languages and the Primary National Curriculum, see, for example, Unit 5, *Growing Things* which links with Science *Sc2 Life processes and living things*. They are available in French, German and Spanish, and comprise 24 discrete units of work, which can be taught from the beginning of Year 3 to the end of Year 6. The Units cover set topics (see Figure 3.1, QCA Schemes of Work for Languages at KS2: Scope of Study). Although the Schemes of Work are non-statutory, they ensure a consistency of provision for languages at KS2, and allow teachers and other practitioners to understand, and plan for progress, from Year 3 to Year 6. Equally, they are a useful collaborative planning tool for primary and secondary teachers to ensure a continuum of language learning from KS2 to KS3. The Schemes of Work are developed without reference to a particular context, thus teachers can adapt the ideas and content to suit their own needs, and those of their pupils. You can purchase a hard copy of the Schemes, or download them from http://www.qca.org.uk/qca_11752.aspx in either PDF or RTF format.

Each unit is structured in the same way. The *key planning features* of each unit are:

- *Title and number of the unit* which are consistent across all languages, and are given in both the target language and in English.
- *Resources* gives ideas for the kinds of materials and resources that will support teaching and learning in the particular unit.
- *About the unit* explains the rationale for the unit, giving clear learning objectives.
- *Where the unit fits in* explains how learning in this unit links to learning across the Scheme of Work.

| 1. | All about me | 13. | Healthy eating |
|----|----|----|----|
| 2. | Games and songs | 14. | I am the music man |
| 3. | Celebrations | 15. | On the way to school |
| 4. | Portraits | 16. | Beach scene |
| 5. | The Four Friends | 17. | The return of Spring |
| 6. | Growing things | 18. | The planets |
| 7. | All aboard | 19. | Our school |
| 8. | Pocket money | 20. | The world about us |
| 9. | Tell me a story! | 21. | Then and now |
| 10. | Our sporting lives | 22. | Out and about |
| 11. | Carnival of the animals | 23. | Creating a café |
| 12. | What's the weather like? | 24. | What's in the news? |

**Figure 3.1**  The QCA Schemes of Work for Languages at KS2: Scope of Study

- *Prior learning* details the knowledge, skill and understanding that should already have been covered to make the most of this unit – 'it is helpful if children already know ...', which in turn provides teachers with valuable guidance in planning for progression.
- *New language* gives details about functions, notions, grammar and structures covered in the unit.
- *Links with other subjects* gives detailed information about cross-curricular links, and identifies how this unit can enhance learning in other specified curriculum areas.
- *Expectations* describes what pupils may be expected to achieve by the end of the unit under headings: 'most children will'; 'some children will have not have made so much progress and will'; 'some children will have progressed further and will' – this can be useful in planning differentiated activities not only within the particular unit, but also in future units.
- *Language* this is given in two parts: *core language* of the unit, which comprises language integral to the entire Scheme of Work and *additional language* which may be encountered in this unit, but not covered explicitly either in this unit, or across the Scheme of Work – again, this can be useful in planning for particularly able pupils.
- *Additional language for teachers* gives information on the range of language and structures that teachers can use to deliver the unit.

The *key content features* of each unit are:

- *Learning sections* – which may number between four and six sections per unit. So, for example, in Unit 11, 'Carnival of the Animals', we have:
  - ○ Section 1 – Meet the animals
  - ○ Section 2 – Animal sounds
  - ○ Section 3 – What's the time?
  - ○ Section 4 – Animal descriptions
  - ○ Section 5 – Animal habitats
  - ○ Section 6 – Carnival time.

- *Learning objectives* for each section, with specific reference to the KS2 Framework for Languages.
- *Possible teaching activities* for each section, giving detailed information about how to structure learning around these activities.
- *Learning outcomes* for each section.
- *Points to note* for each section which gives additional information such as how to locate resources on the web, biographical information, song lyrics, follow-up activities, and so on.
- *End of unit activities* ideas for unit 'plenaries', bringing learning together.

## Activity

With reference to the National Curriculum – Handbook for Primary Teachers in England (www.nc.uk.net) and a unit from the QCA Scheme of Work, map out possible cross-curricular links that you can embed into your language programme.

Example: *Unit 6 – Growing things*

### Literacy

- using knowledge of phonics to experiment with possible spellings of new/ unfamiliar words;
- storytelling (Jack and the Beanstalk);
- understanding how verbs work;
- presenting ideas;
- ordering sentences to describe events.

### Science

- life processes common to plants, including growth, nutrition and reproduction;
- make links between life processes in familiar plants and the environments in which they are found;
- nutrition and the need for food for activity and growth, and about the importance of an adequate and varied diet for health;
- cultivate and monitor the growth of small plants in the classroom;
- gather evidence, collect and present data.

*Art & Design*

- design posters about healthy eating for display in the classroom or school;
- design a brochure for a local garden centre;
- create a greengrocer stall in the classroom, with models of fruit and vegetables;
- take digital images of the plants being cultivated in the classroom at each stage of growth.

*ICT*

- carry out a survey on healthy eating and present findings in a spreadsheet;
- keep an electronic healthy eating diary;
- use digital photographs, clipart and other images to create a page for the school website on the growing process of the classroom plants.

## Examples of the Framework in action: understanding progression in language learning across KS2

The Framework offers an invaluable template for planning for progression. At the end of each Year Group section, there is a table outlining learning outcomes per strand, with relevant learning activities. Look at the following selection of objectives from Yrs 3 to 6 to give you some idea of how pupils may progress across KS2, and how teachers can facilitate that progression:

# Oracy

*Year 3*

3.1  Listen and respond to simple rhymes, stories and songs
3.4  Listen attentively and understand instructions, everyday classroom language and praise words

*Year 6*

6.1  Understand the main points and simple opinions in a spoken story, song or passage
6.4  Use spoken language confidently to initiate and sustain conversations and to tell stories

# Literacy

*Year 3*

3.1  Recognize some familiar words in written form
3.3  Experiment with the writing of simple words

*Year 6*

6.1 Read and understand the main points and some details from a short written passage
6.3 Match sound to sentences and paragraphs

## Intercultural understanding

*Year 3*

3.1 Learn about the different languages spoken by children in the school
3.2 Locate country/countries where the language is spoken

*Year 6*

6.2 Recognize and understand some of the differences between people
6.3 Present information about an aspect of culture

## Knowledge about language

*Year 3*

• Notice the spelling of familiar words
• Recognize that many languages are spoken in the UK and across the world
• Words will not always have a direct equivalent in the language

*Year 6*

• Recognize patterns in the foreign language
• Devise questions for authentic use

## Language learning strategies

*Year 3*

• Discuss language learning and share ideas and experiences
• Compare the language with English

*Year 6*

• Plan and prepare – analyse what needs to be done in order to carry out a task
• Use context and previous knowledge to help understanding and previous skills

## Ensuring progression in language learning: using the Attainment Targets (ATs)

The Attainment Targets in language teaching and learning refer to four particular language skills, and can provide both teachers and pupils with a useful template for planning for progression in language learning (see Chapter 2 for links between the ATs and the National Curriculum for English, and Chapter 5 for further discussion on how to use Attainment Targets to promote Assessment for Learning in the languages classroom).

---

## Four Key Language Skills: The Attainment Targets

Attainment Target 1: Listening and responding
Attainment Target 2: Speaking
Attainment Target 3: Reading and responding
Attainment Target 4: Writing

---

Each AT is scoped across eight discrete levels, with a ninth for 'exceptional performance'. Traditionally, we work across Levels 1–4 in primary languages, though it is reasonable to assume that many pupils will be able to achieve a Level 5 by the end of Year 6 if they have followed a structured programme of language learning since Year 3. The key difference between Levels 1–4 and Level 5 is the ability to recognize and use the past and future tenses, as well as the present.

As you plan units of work, and individual lessons, refer to the ATs as a roadmap for progression. Box 3.2 shows how it is possible to increase challenge, and to promote a more involved engagement with language throughout the four levels of AT1: Listening and responding. There are three important points to remember as you plan with reference to ATs:

1    In order for a pupil to 'achieve' a particular level, he/she should be performing consistently at that level.
2    It is reasonable to include elements of a higher level within work centred around the current level in order to encourage pupils to engage with language actively, rather than to get into the habit of responding only to learned prompts.
3    In terms of AT1 (listening and responding) and AT3 (reading and responding), be very clear about how you intend pupils to 'respond'. For example, if pupils are given a short written text to read, in what way is it appropriate for them to respond? There are a variety of choices: verbally, in English; verbally, in the target language (which means you are also working on AT2, speaking); identifying correct responses by ticking picture or written boxes; in writing, either in English or the target language (which means you are also working on AT4, writing). Responding in the target language also means that you have to consider the extent to which *accuracy*, either in spoken or written language, will inform your judgement on whether a pupil has achieved a particular level. Generally, it is acknowledged that language

learners progress at different paces in different skills, so it is possible for a pupil to understand the spoken word, respond appropriately *but with little accuracy* – yet still be deemed to have achieved a particular level in listening and reading.

---

## Box 3.2 Progressing learning with Attainment Targets

**Level 1:** Pupils show that they understand a few familiar spoken words and phrases. They understand speech spoken clearly, face to face or from a good quality recording. They may need a lot of help, such as repetition or gesture.
- responding appropriately to the register;
- responding appropriately to classroom instructions by the teacher;
- responding appropriately to simple prompts such as 'Hello, how are you?'

**Level 2:** Pupils show that they understand a range of familiar spoken phrases. They respond to a clear model of standard language, but may need items to be repeated.
- responding appropriately to simple questions such as 'What is your name?', 'How old are you?', 'Where do you live?', 'What is the weather like today?'

**Level 3:** Pupils show that they understand the main points from short spoken passages made up of familiar language. They identify and note personal responses. They may need short sections to be repeated.
- engaging appropriately in brief conversational exchanges, rather than individual set question and answer sequences;
- responding appropriately to questions based on language spoken or read by the teacher, or via an audiovisual resource, either in English or the target language.

**Level 4:** Pupils show that they understand the main points and some of the detail from spoken passage made up of familiar language in simple sentences. They may need some items to be repeated.
- engaging appropriately in more complex conversational exchanges;
- responding appropriately, with increased detail, to questions based on language spoken or read by the teacher, or via an audiovisual resource, either in English or the target language.

**Level 5:** Pupils show they understand the main points and opinions in spoken passages made up of familiar material from various contexts, including present, past or future events. They made need some repetition.
- engaging appropriately in more complex conversational exchanges which do not focus solely on the present;
- responding appropriately, with increased detail, to questions based on language spoken or read by the teacher, or via an audiovisual resource, either in English or the target language;
- identifying when language describes events that *will* happen and *have* happened.

# Teachers talking

## The Framework in action – intercultural understanding and cross-curricular teaching and learning in Year 4 German

A teacher describes how he adapted framework objectives, and used them to plan a sequence of activities for his Year 4 group:

> Essentially, I use the Framework as an ideas bank – it's full of them. We do need guidance in primary languages, and I think it's important that practitioners are singing from largely the same hymn sheet. I don't actually always stick to the Year 4 objectives – I move in and out of them, according to where I think the pupils are in their learning, and what they'll respond to. I was really keen to involve the pupils themselves in drawing up a programme of learning, so we looked at the objectives and brainstormed the kinds of things we could do. I built in cross-curricular learning too – firstly with literacy – each pupil had to prepare a short presentation on their favourite children's story and we created a display from that. When we started to explore popular German children's stories we chose *Der Struwelpeter* by Heinrich Hoffmann as they are really something that children can relate to – all those consequences for misbehaving! The beauty of that collection of stories is that it is available in English too – my German's quite good – I've got a Grade A at A Level – but I like to be sure I get all the nuances and so on. We linked both Citizenship – and Science to this theme as well – our linked topic was 'World Citizens: Caring for our Environment' – when we looked at the various ways to travel to Germany, we talked about the different nationalities and religions that make up modern Germany, and which was the least environmentally damaging way of getting there. I managed to get in a fair bit of maths too by allocating small groups of pupils different amounts of pounds, which they had to exchange for euros, and get to Germany with. They had to survive there for three days too. We used Wikipedia and www.google.de to find out information, and to plot our journeys. What was really interesting was looking at supermarket websites, trying to buy food – they were absolutely shocked at what food costs, particularly the less healthy kind! There's a Struwelpeter Museum in Frankfurt which has a lovely website – the German is generally too advanced for the class, but we worked out entrance prices, opening times and so on, and did some interesting ICT activities like saving the images of the museum and using them in a little leaflet about it we designed. We also created a poster outlining our objectives – we've translated 'intercultural understanding' to 'interkulturelle Verständigung' – and linked it to our normal practice of WALT (we are learning to ...). This familiarity – you know, using methods in languages that we use across the curriculum, really works well.

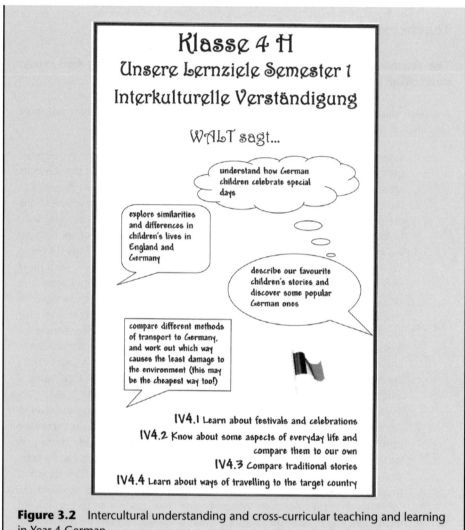

**Figure 3.2** Intercultural understanding and cross-curricular teaching and learning in Year 4 German

## Beginning to plan: short, medium and longer term

Planning primary languages programmes, units of work and lessons rests on the same principles of practice as other areas across the curriculum. As we discussed in Chapter 2, there are fundamental principles to effective learning and teaching in the primary phase and these likewise underpin primary languages practice.

*Excellence and Enjoyment: Learning and Teaching in the Primary Years – Designing Opportunities for Learning* (DfES 2004c) defines the distinction between short-term, medium-term and long-term planning as follows:

- A *short-term plan* covers a week, a day or a lesson, and consists of the working notes or the structure and content of a planned activity. These may contain details of key questions to ask, teaching strategies and resources, differentiation and assessment opportunities. (Some teachers include some of these items in medium-term plans. The exact balance between the detail in medium- and short-term plans is something to be decided at school level.)
- A *medium-term plan* is usually a planned sequence of work for a subject or area of learning for a period of several weeks, such as a half-term or term. Medium-term planning focuses on organizing coherent units of work around clustered learning objectives and their outcome(s) and on the learning experiences that will enable these to be achieved.
- A *long-term plan* usually shows the planned programme of work for each subject or area of learning for a year group. Long-term plans will often be brought together to cover ages phases (e.g. science from Year 3 to Year 6).

(DfES 2004c: 19)

## Creating an appropriate lesson plan template for KS2 languages

The key to ensuring quality teaching and learning in your lesson is thinking carefully about the template within which you will actually plan for that teaching and learning. While some schools have a 'universal' template, which all staff are required to use, you may find that you will have to adapt that template slightly for your languages lessons.

---

### Activity

#### Step 1

*A template for lesson planning*: In small groups, discuss what you consider to be the strengths and/or weaknesses of Lesson Plans 1 and 2 on pp. 44–7. Reflect particularly on the particular section headings – to what extent do these contribute meaningfully to sound planning? Design a template which incorporates what you have identified as key features of an effective lesson plan, and present it to the whole group, articulating clearly the rationale for your design.

### Step 2

*The content and structure of an effective lesson plan*: look carefully at the content and structure of each lesson plan, and visualize the lesson they refer to. Consider the following questions:

- Is the lesson, and therefore the intended learning, meaningful?
- Are the plans sufficiently detailed to enable you to understand each stage of the lesson in terms of both teacher and pupil activity?
- Would you be able to teach the lesson successfully from the plan? Why/not?

## Lesson Plan 1

| Learner Group | Ability Range | Date | Time |
|---|---|---|---|
| Yr 5 | 1 G&T; 2 SEN (English); 2 EAL (Urdu, Polish first language); mixed | 4.02.07 | Period 2, Thursday 10–10.50 (50 mins) |

**Topic** A trip to France (over 6 lessons, 3rd lesson in SoW)

**Context**
- Combining likes/dislikes/interests with some cultural input on France
- Promoting language for authentic purposes; none of the children have been to France but we're preparing for our first communication with a new partner school
- Encourage increased use of TL
- Homework from last lesson: prepare short presentation or PPT max 5 mins on their chosen area of France

**Learning Objectives**
- Increased use of spoken TL; confidence-building
- Embed previously learnt linguistic structures
- Information sharing re. France (self-study)
- ICT/research/study skills

## Materials/Resources/Technology

- PPT with lesson overview
- Word document with 2 x role-play
- IWB screening www.google.fr/bordeaux; www.wikipedia.com

## T&L Activities

- 10.00–10.05 – recap last lesson; discuss today's objectives, remind them to jot down any new words in rough for *carnet de vocabulaire*
- 10.05–10.15 – starter: bingo with pays francophones x 2
- 10.15–10.20 – discussion in English re. homework; how they found facts, etc.
- 10.20–10.30 – with partner, practise presentation in TL; go round observing
- 10.30–10.45 – 2 x presentations (volunteers)
- 10.45–10.50 – plenary, review of objectives, pack up

## Homework/Self-study

- Write up new words in *carnet de vocabulaire*

## Assessment Opportunities

- Formative: monitor participation in group and pair work; particular emphasis today on verbal input
- More formal approach: take in presentations to mark – emphasis on range of language and accuracy

## Differentiation

- By outcome (e.g. presentation guidelines)
- EAL – additional support in class time

## Evaluation

More input required on 'what makes a good presentation?' – some pupils still very unsure; all keen to talk in the TL; library/dictionary skills need working on – too much reliance on internet and *carnet de vocabulaire* not up-to-date – some pupils struggling with bilingual dictionary.

## Lesson Plan 2

| Class 4G | Subject French | Lesson Number 3 | Unit Number 2 |
|---|---|---|---|
| Number in Class 25 | SEN 3 | G&T | EAL 7 |

| | |
|---|---|
| **Learning Objectives**<br><br><br><br>**Learning Outcomes** | To be able to say where you live, and where it is; to ask someone where they live, to understand the response, and be able to report back; to revise key European countries/capitals (working towards O4.4); to create short dialogues/texts on this subject (L4.4)<br>Pupils will be able to engage in simple descriptive conversation about their home town, and key European countries/capitals, using simple Q&A techniques and tell other people about the information they have gathered about each other |
| **Key Words/ Phrases** | Où habites-tu? J'habite à/en<br>C'est où exactement? Dans le nord/sud/ouest/est de . . .<br>Dans le nord-ouest/sud-ouest/nord-est/sud-est de . . .<br>l'Angleterre/Londres; La France/Paris; La Belgique/Bruxelles; La Suisse/Berne; L'Allemagne/Berlin; L'Espagne/Madrid; L'Italie/Rome; Le Portugal/Lisbonne; L'Ecosse/Edimbourg; République d'Irlande/Dublin; Le Pays de Galles/Cardiff |
| **Starter (5 mins)** | In two teams, with points: Oral spelling – quel pays commence avec un 'I'?, quelle capitale commence avec un 'P'?; written spelling – start writing words on the board, pupils shout out what they think the word is – deduct point for wrong answer! (O4.3, L4.3) |
| **Activities** | 1  10 minutes – give out match worksheet – play MP3 file, pupils tick the box according to what they hear – tell them to listen very carefully because we'll be trying to recreate the conversations (O4.2)<br>2  10 minutes: Whole-group: put together a conversation like the model they heard in the MP3 file<br>3  5 minutes: pair work: practise Q&A according to first two activities<br>4  5–10 minutes: volunteers for performance at the front of the class (O4.1) |

| | |
|---|---|
| **Plenary** | *5–10 minutes plenary: rota pupil to summarize what we've learnt; quick-fire Q&A teacher-lead, finish with pre-written bingo sheets using countries/capitals* |
| **Homework:** | *Give out exemplar written conversations – create an identity, e.g. Pierre, age, where he lives – bonus points for other conversation they can add from previous lessons (max 30 minutes) – in homework books (L4.1, L4.4)* |
| **Differentiation** | *All pupils are able to engage with the lesson; additional support during listening activity and pair work by moving around, giving advice or clues; extension activity – given in homework – increased complexity in written exemplars, with some dictionary work involved; less text/bigger font and less complex task for SEN; EAL extra reference sheet* |
| **Assessment** | *Observation during lesson, marked homework, pupil response during plenary* |
| **Resources** | *MP3 file and IWB; matching worksheets; scrap paper for jotting ideas down/remembering dialogue; homework sheets* |
| **TA/LSA** | *To move around the class during the entire lesson, giving advice, support and encouragement where she feels it is needed with particular focus on the 3SEN/7EAL* |
| **Cross-curricular opportunities** | *Geographical understanding; directions/compass points*<br>*Literacy: reading/writing homework*<br>*Oracy: listening/speaking focus during lesson* |
| **Post-lesson evaluation** | *Increase number of countries/capitals for more able pupils, giving extension worksheets – use more complex maps*<br>*No longer than 10 minutes for whole-group discussion – I allowed this one to go on too long*<br>*Needed longer than 5 minutes to make the most of the plenary* |

## Trainees talking

In terms of section headings, we preferred Lesson Plan 2 because it highlights the key elements of a good lesson – so it made us think not only about the actual language being taught – and then how this would fit into a medium-term plan, but about how we'd structure the lesson itself with a starter, main section and then plenary. The timings are useful, as this allows you to map out your lesson and think about what each activity actually entails. We thought that specifying cross-curricular opportunities was a good idea, as when it comes to doing a curriculum map, and explicitly linking learning, you have really vital information to hand. It's a bit dense though – we found Lesson Plan 1 far easier to read. Both of them include a box for evaluation which is really important on teaching practice. We think the section for core language is absolutely vital to new practitioners, and really helps you map out progression in the medium and longer term. Obviously differentiation and assessment opportunities need to be in your plan, not only because Ofsted look at that very closely, but because we can't really plan for progression in learning, or set realistic or appropriate challenges unless we support learning appropriately.

Well, we generally thought that Lesson Plan 2 would be the easiest to teach from – it has lots of detail, and you can see exactly what's being taught and why. The learning objectives are well defined, and we thought they're very reasonable. There are also clear links to the Framework, which is useful. We did question though how realistic it is to expect teachers to plan each and every lesson in this kind of detail – maybe on teaching practice we have to, but in general, we don't think we'd have time when we've got a full timetable. We agreed that there has to be a certain level of detail in order to visualize the lesson, and to situate it within the medium-term plan – and also to share with, or generally guide less experienced colleagues. The objectives in both plans were really clear, and you can see immediately from them what the lesson is all about – why the teacher is actually doing this.

## Box 3.3 Observations and reflections on lesson planning

As you review your lesson plans, refer to the following checklist for effective primary languages planning:

### Planning
Are my learning objectives well-defined and reasonable?
- Am I using ICT appropriately?
- Am I challenging individual learners appropriately?

- Am I planning effectively for TA input in supporting learning?
- How am I planning for cross-curricular links?
- In what ways am I enhancing literacy and oracy skills, and using pupils' knowledge and understanding of their own language to support the TL?
- Am I planning appropriate use of the TL?
- Am I including an intercultural or cultural awareness element to my lesson?
- Is the balance between the four skills appropriate?
- How am I timing individual activities?
- Am I including an appropriate range of activities?
- Are my resources appropriate and visually attractive?
- Am I planning for progression in learning?

## Assessment
- How am I feeding back to pupils as part of my formative assessment strategy?
- How well am I embedding AfL strategies into teaching and learning?
- Am I using assessment to inform future planning?

## Teaching and class management
- Do my pupils understand the learning objectives?
- Is my use of ICT supporting learning?
- To what extent am I enhancing pupils' skills in other areas of the curriculum, such as literacy, numeracy, humanities, ICT?
- Am I using the TL appropriately?
- Am I maximizing opportunity for pupil use of the TL?
- Am I modelling good pronunciation and use of the TL?
- Am I encouraging pupils to think about how they learn most effectively, and to understand the nature of language?
- Am I encouraging individual, pair, small and whole-group work, and weighting them appropriately?
- Are my differentiation strategies adequate?
- Am I challenging all learners effectively?
- Am I supporting SEN/EAL effectively?

## Activity

Choose a unit from the QCA Schemes of Work, and using your preferred lesson plan template, plan a 45-minute lesson for a Year 5 group of 28 pupils of mixed ability. Present your lesson plan to the group, explaining its rationale, and the content/ structure of your lesson. As you begin to plan, ask yourself the three 'key questions' in planning for learning:

1    What am I trying to achieve?
2    How do I organize learning?
3    How well am I achieving my aims?
A fourth key question to consider is:
4    How am I measuring to what extent my aims are being achieved?
Explain to the group exactly how you might measure if your lesson aims are being achieved.

## Planning for the medium term

In order to ensure effective medium-term planning, it is essential to establish the following issues:

- How many lessons are there per week, and how long are those lessons? (Remember that the Framework recommends a minimum of 60 minutes per week in curriculum time.)
- How many lessons will there be per term, particularly Autumn term, when curriculum time is often involved with whole-school Christmas activities? When you have this information you can scope content across a half-term and term, and thus ultimately across a whole year (long-term).
- Are there any specific longer-term Year Group projects in other curriculum areas that may mean some lessons do not take place?
- Who will be delivering the lessons? Remember that the particular expertise of the teachers, both in terms of subject knowledge and teaching, will impact upon what you can expect them to deliver.
- What do you know about the prior attainment of your pupils? In order to plan appropriately in terms of differentiation and challenge, you need to know about the pupils actually being taught.

## Activity

Look carefully at Figure 3.3 A template for medium-term planning. In small groups, choose a Unit of Work from the QCA Schemes of Work and adapt its content according to six lessons of 30 minutes each. As you plan, consider to what with particular reference to progression in language learning and cross-curricular learning. You will find it useful to refer to your Primary National Curriculum Handbook also.

| Timescale: | | Number of Lessons: | | Ref: QCA SoW Unit | |
|---|---|---|---|---|---|
| Unit No: 1 | Framework Objectives covered in Unit | Unit Objectives | | | |
| Prior learning (give brief detail) | | | | | |
| Cross-curricular Learning | | | Context | | |
| Core Language | | | | | |
| | Language | Cross-curricular learning | Teacher and pupil activities | | Framework Objectives |
| Lesson 1 | | | | | |
| Lesson 2 | | | | | |
| Lesson 3 | | | | | |
| Lesson 4 | | | | | |
| Lesson 5 | | | | | |
| Lesson 6 | | | | | |
| Out-of-school learning<br>Lesson 1<br>Lesson 2<br>Lesson 3<br>Lesson 4<br>Lesson 5<br>Lesson 6 | | | | | |
| Display and Project Work | | | | | |
| Assessment Opportunities | | | | | |
| Assessment for Learning Strategies | | | | | |
| Strategies for Differentiation | | | | | |
| LSA/TA Support? YES/NO – details of support skillset | | | | | |
| Attainment Targets: Levels 2–3: summary of key strategies<br>Developing listening and responding skills<br>Developing speaking skills<br>Developing reading and responding skills<br>Developing writing skills | | | | | |
| End of Unit Activity/Assessment | | | | | |
| Post-unit Evaluation | | | | | |
| Objectives achieved | Objectives to be revisited | Attainment Targets achieved | Any additional language used | | Pupil opinions – give brief details |

**Figure 3.3**   A template for medium-term planning

## Planning for the longer term

As you begin to plan for the longer term, refer in the first instance to the overview provided at the beginning of each Year Group section of the Framework (see Figure 3.4) as well as the detailed guidance on how to integrate cross-curricular learning effectively in Part 3 of the Framework. This will give you a sense of how to structure content, and plan particular teaching and learning activities. Remember that you may use the Framework very flexibly, according to the current programme of provision in your school. You can use these to plot content and teaching and learning activities across both individual Year Groups and the whole of KS2. Refer to your school curriculum map to help you understand ways of meaningfully integrating language teaching and learning across the curriculum.

Currently, schools are gradually beginning to develop meaningful approaches to long-term planning which situates languages firmly within the whole-school vision for teaching and learning, and we anticipate that within 4–5 years, most schools will have successfully integrated languages into the whole-school curriculum map.

---

### Teachers talking

#### Integrating languages into whole-school curriculum mapping

A Year 4 Primary German teacher talks about developments in his school:

> Now that I've got a pretty structured German programme in place, which maps learning across the whole of KS2, the Governors, the Head and all the staff in fact can see how it really contributes to children's learning, and engages and motivates them, and, you know, actually teaches them something about the language and culture of a really close neighbour as well, so it really is one of those win-win situations – so, that's convinced everyone that we'll get even more out of it if really explicit links are made across the year groups in content and skills-based work. I don't mind if that means I eventually have to adapt my current programme – primary languages, in fact, the entire curriculum, really does work best when it's done as an integrated, joined-up thinking programme of learnng. Children themselves make explicit links, and often say 'Oh yeah, we did that in maths or English, so we can try it out here or change it a bit and do it this way in German.' We've had several meetings just to scope our first steps – I keep telling everyone we should experiment, and keep the map under really tight review, and I'm convinced within a couple of years we'll have a map that will help us structure and really integrate learning across the curriculum, where German plays as important a role in that learning as everything else – can't you tell I'm a big fan?

---

| Expectations | Outcomes |
|---|---|
| During Year 3 | By the end of year 3, most children should be able to: |
| **Oracy**<br>At the beginning of Year 3 the main emphasis is on familiarising children with the sounds and speech patterns of the new language. They enjoy listening to and joining in with a range of songs, poems and stories, and develop their confidence, imagination and self-expression.<br><br>They learn to differentiate unfamiliar sounds and words. They mimic and play with sounds. They understand simple words and phrases, and begin to repeat and to use some of them independently in simple communicative tasks and role-plays.<br><br>They listen to a variety of voices, which may include the class teacher, visiting native speakers, audio CDs, cassettes and use websites and CD-ROMs, DVDs or videos. | • Enjoy listening to and speaking in the language<br>• Listen and respond to familiar spoken words, phrases and sentences<br>• Communicate with others using simple words and phrases and short sentences<br>• Understand conventions such as taking turns to speak, valuing the contribution of others<br>• Use correct pronunciation in spoken work. |
| **Literacy**<br>As children listen to sounds, words and phrases, they repeat and chorus, learning accurate pronunciation. They then gradually learn to link simple phonemes and spellings. They enjoy reading a few familiar words and phrases aloud and begin to write letters and familiar words. They also experiment with writing some familiar words from memory. | • Recognise and understand some familiar words and phrases in written form<br>• Read aloud in chorus, with confidence and enjoyment, from a known text<br>• Write some familiar simple words using a model<br>• Write some familiar words from memory. |
| **Intercultural Understanding**<br>Learning a language arouses children's interest and curiosity in their own identities and helps them to see the relationships between their lives and those of others. During the year they think about the linguistic diversity of their own school and talk about the languages they would like to learn. They find out where the language they are learning is spoken.<br><br>They make contact either in person or through Internet or video with a partner school or native speaker, e.g. a parent, or a language assistant. | • Appreciate the diversity of languages spoken within their school<br>• Talk about the similarities and differences of social conventions between different cultures<br>• Identify the country or countries where the language is spoken<br>• Have some contact with the country/countries<br>• Recognise a children's song, rhyme or poem well known to native speakers. |
| **KAL and LLS**<br>At this initial stage, children begin to foster their interest in the similarities and differences between languages and begin to think together about how they are learning the new language. | |

**Figure 3.4**  Expectations and outcomes at Year 3, DfES 2005

## Activity

### Part 1

In small groups, brainstorm ideas for activities that will address both expectations and outcomes at Year 3. Discuss your ideas as a whole group, and then decide to what extent the same activities may be appropriate for another Year Group, and in what ways you might raise the level of cognitive challenge appropriately.

### Part 2

Using the template given in Figure 3.3, outline the ideas and content of a possible year-long plan for a Year Group of your choice, using both the Framework and QCA Schemes of Work for reference.

### Part 3

In pairs, choose one of the activities discussed in Part 1. Prepare the activity as a 15-minute micro-teaching demonstration for both Year 3, and for Year 6. As a whole group, discuss the key differences you identified when preparing similar content for Year 3 and Year 6.

## Short-term, medium-term and longer-term planning: the cycle of effective primary languages planning

We have discussed in some detail the features of effective lesson – or short-term – planning. As you develop as a primary languages practitioner, you will begin to implement medium-term and longer-term planning into your overall planning strategy. As we saw above, you should use the QCA Schemes of Work to inform your planning, and to help you visualize how your primary languages programmes can develop across year groups, and thus the whole school.

Ofsted (2002) characterized features of effective practice in planning including:

- medium-term and short-term plans are detailed and complement each other;
- subject headings from long-term plans inform learning objectives;
- well-defined and clear objectives shared with pupils;
- adopting a three-part lesson structure, including clear introduction and plenary where appropriate;
- engaging in lively, interactive direct teaching.

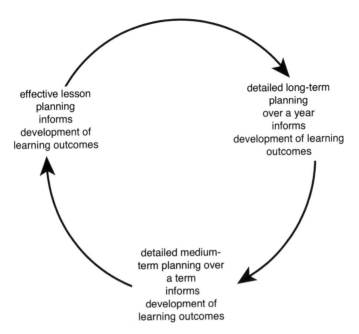

**Figure 3.5**  The cycle of effective planning

Thus, the tri-partite and cyclical approach to planning – long, medium and short term, contributes to a comprehensive and coherent map of learning across a particular year group, and ultimately across the whole school. Equally important is the systematic and iterative *review* of planning, which informs future development – monitoring achievement of learning outcomes, and evaluating the effectiveness of both teaching and learning. Figure 3.5 illustrates the cycle of effective planning.

# Working successfully with a teaching or foreign language assistant

## The Teaching or Learning Support Assistant (TA/LSA)

Teaching or learning support assistants have become valued members of the primary community, and are an invaluable resource to the teacher, the pupils and the school as a whole. In planning, it is essential that we engage teaching assistants, direct their skills appropriately to support pupil learning, and contribute in part to their overall professional development. Each assistant will bring a different skillset to the primary languages classroom, and you should take steps to investigate where their skills and interests lie. In terms of your own professional development, this relates directly to the following standards:

- Communicating and working with others:
  Q6: have a commitment to collaboration and cooperative working
- Team working and collaboration:
  Ensure that colleagues working with them are appropriately involved in supporting learning and understand the roles they are expected to fulfil.

(TDA 2007)

It may be that a teaching assistant is available to support a particular pupil or set of pupils, rather than the learning of the entire class, and it is important for you to understand in advance the precise role of the assistant. Ask the member of staff responsible for allocating learning support for information on the role of individual assistants, and equally importantly, for a timetable outlining when you will have an assistant with you.

### What should primary languages teaching assistants know?

In order to support learning meaningfully, teaching assistants need to be aware not only of what they have to do within an individual lesson, and have the necessary skills to do so, but they require a sound understanding of the framework within which learning is taking place. Thus, teaching assistants should have a working knowledge of:

- the language being taught;
- the aims and objectives of the KS2 Framework for Languages;
- the QCA Schemes of Work for Modern Languages at KS2;
- how language learning can support and enhance learning in other areas of the curriculum;
- the resources and materials available for language teaching;
- language teaching and learning strategies.

### The foreign language assistant (FLA)

Clearly, the FLA will have a different skillset to that of the TA/LSA. While they have a mastery of their native language, their English skills may not be particularly strong.

### What should primary FLAs know?

Given that FLAs are often languages undergraduates, or ERASMUS exchange students, it is not necessarily the case that you will have an FLA who is a trainee teacher. Even where your FLA is training to be a teacher in his or her home country, bear in mind that teaching practices may differ quite considerably from accepted practice here in the UK. The length of stay can vary from a short number of weeks to a whole year. Where the TA/LSA will have an understanding of the English education system, the ways that primary schools work, and the general stage of learning that pupils have reached, the FLAs will not necessarily share the same understanding. Thus, there are several underpinning principles that FLAs need to know:

- brief detail prior learning across the curriculum;
- the level of language that pupils are able to understand;
- the overall objectives of particular units of work;
- the role of lesson planning, and their role within that process;
- their role within the learning process – perhaps in the form of a job specification.

### Effective planning with a TA/LSA or FLA

There are several important areas to consider in order to ensure that you are planning effectively for a TA/LSA or FLA. First, you need to inform yourself about their general skillset, interests, experience, background, training and qualifications. In the case of the TA/LSA, what is their level of competence in the target language? For the FLA, what is their level of competence in English? Is he/she a trainee teacher? What is his/her understanding of primary practice in England? Are they competent in standard ICT resources such as the interactive whiteboard? Are they aware of health and safety issues? You should plan time to explain the overall vision for languages in your school, as well as to involve assistants directly in the planning process – they will have a lot of ideas to contribute, and in this way will be able to take more ownership of their professional activity within the languages lessons. Likewise, you should ideally find time to involve the assistants directly in the evaluation process – they may have seen or noticed things that you haven't, and will have formed their own opinions about how individual pupils are engaging with learning, particularly where they are working with a designated pupil or set of pupils. Make sure that the assistants have a copy of your long-term and medium-term plan. These plans will enable them to situate learning within the broader framework, and understand the underpinning principles of the learning programme. It is also essential that you provide the assistants with a copy of your lesson plan in advance of the lesson so that they can prepare themselves appropriately, and ensure that your instructions for their input are sufficiently explicit. You will find it useful to discuss with other colleagues how they plan for the effective deployment of assistants.

## Foreign Languages Assistant talking

I'm in my final year of training to be a primary teacher in North Germany, and was really pleased to have the opportunity to work in an English primary school. I wanted to improve my English, but also to understand the ways that teachers teach, and compare how children learn, in Germany and England. My responsibilities included working in all the classes to support the teachers in their German teaching, as well as being involved in literacy and numeracy.

I had to plan those lessons very carefully to be sure I knew exactly what had to be taught, and the language I would need to teach it. We had regular meetings, and I would suggest words and phrases, and information about how we teach languages in Germany that the teachers could try out. What I found difficult at first was not knowing exactly how the school worked, and also getting used to the interactive whiteboard, as we do not use these so much in my region. The teachers here do use the interactive whiteboard very much, and I can see that this can be a very valuable teaching aid. I don't think it is necessary to have a PowerPoint for every lesson, as sometimes I prefer to concentrate on listening and communicating personally. I plan my lessons very carefully, but we do not focus too much on long-term planning, and for English we use a set textbook, which we follow. It was very interesting to see how the teachers in England plan over many weeks, and I can see exactly what they wish to achieve in a whole term. The teachers also create many of their own resources, which I think does add to the planning time. I often worked with small groups of children, and concentrated on pronunciation and speaking. The children were always interested in my stories about Germany, and I showed them many pictures I have of my country, and of schools I have worked in. They loved to see and talk about German primary schools. The teachers always involved me in planning, and I think my stay here [for four weeks] was so successful because I felt like a real part of the team. I have remained in contact with my school, and am working with my English mentor on creating what we have called a 'learning relationship' between our pupils. We all feel this is very important as it makes German real, and not just another school subject.

For additional information, consult the British Council on www.britishcouncil.org. The Council produces a very useful information pack for FLAs, and for schools, and this is an equally valuable resource for TAs: The *Primary FLA Starter Pack* includes an interesting selection of teaching tips and ideas, as well as images for use with flashcards.

## Conclusion

Effective planning takes place within a wider framework of curriculum planning: long-, medium- and short-term planning are part of a cyclical interrelated process and inform the development of learning programmes across the whole school, and the whole curriculum. Effective practitioners reflect carefully on the stated aims and outcomes of learning, ensuring that they are both reasonable, and achievable. For pupils to participate fully in the teaching and learning process, objectives must be clearly defined, and relevant to their context. As we discuss in this chapter, and elsewhere in the book, best practice in primary languages planning is achieved through a holistic approach to planning, and by working within a whole-school vision for *learning*.

Planning for learning is one of the most important skills a teacher has to develop in order to be an effective practitioner. Using the Framework and other curriculum documents is not only enshrined in the new Professional Standards for Teachers, but also enables the language teaching community to work across a nationally recognized template, and thus ensure a level of consistency of provision.

# 4 Teaching and learning strategies for the classroom

---

This chapter discusses:

- strategies for enhancing literacy and oracy skills in the primary languages class-room
- presenting and practising new language
- teacher and pupil language
- creating opportunities for communication in the target language in the classroom
- sequencing a primary languages lesson
- embedding languages into school routines
- supporting learning through classroom and school display
- inclusive practice in the primary languages classroom.

---

## Introduction

As we have already discussed, one of the key objectives of primary language is to support learning in other areas of the curriculum, with a particular emphasis on oracy and literacy. The KS2 Framework offers the following guidance:

> Children spend much of their time in language lessons speaking, listening and interacting – more than in most other subjects. They take part in role-plays, conversations and question and answer work, sing songs and recite, perform to an audience and respond to a wide range of aural stimuli. This emphasis on communication, including language learning's important role in the 'education of the ear', underpins children's capabilities in oracy, which is critical to effective communication as well as a key foundation for literacy.
> (http://www.standards.dfes.gov.uk/primary/publications/languages/
> languages_guidance/pns_mflpart2_190505_pll.pdf, p4)

We would argue that the acquisition of a new language in a classroom setting works best when all key language competences – listening, speaking, reading and writing – are carefully blended to provide a *whole language experience*. Kirsch likewise makes this point, commenting that 'According to theories of SLA [second language acquisition], comprehensible input provided through listening and reading is essential' (2008: 117). Certainly, KS2 pupils, particularly those in upper KS2, are becoming increasingly sophisticated in their use of English, particularly in terms of how they express themselves verbally, in what they read, and in what they are required to write. In order to provide pupils with an appropriate cognitive and meta-linguistic challenge, teachers need to move away from rote learning and word-level work, and allow pupils an opportunity to experiment with language, to test it, and to produce it. This point resonates in part with the recent Ofsted finding that 'Higher attaining pupils, particularly pupils with high levels of literacy, were not always challenged enough' (2008: 10). It should be noted, however, that pupils of all abilities can be encouraged to use and practise both oracy and literacy skills in the target language.

## Strategies for developing literacy skills

The effective primary languages practitioner calls on core teaching competences to ensure a rounded and successful language learning experience. Hall and Hardin identified a range of strategies employed by effective teachers of literacy:

> [They] have a wide and varied repertoire of teaching practices and approaches (e.g. scaffolding, where support in learning is initially provided by the teacher and then gradually withdrawn as the pupils gains in confidence), integrating reading with writing, differentiated instruction, excellent classroom management skills) and they can intelligently and skilfully blend them together in different combinations according to the needs of individual pupils ... they balance direct skills teaching with more authentic, contextually-grounded literacy activities.
>
> (2003: 3)

They noted, 'the early years as a key time for literacy learning; differentiated instruction; authentic opportunities for reading, writing and talk; cross-curricular connections; and careful monitoring of pupils' literacy learning by teachers' (2003: 4). Thus, practitioners new to language teaching should think in terms of how current teaching and learning activities can be meaningfully adapted to the languages classroom, rather than solely in terms of developing a repertoire of entirely new strategies. The current study being undertaken by the DCSF (Cable et al. 2008) recently reported that

> Older children used a good range of top down strategies to work out the meanings of simple language texts in the primary language. However, most children ... often drew on English pronunciation when reading aloud. In most schools children were not confident about writing in the target language. At present, therefore, in the study school children's oracy skills in primary languages are stronger than their literacy abilities. However, some schools demonstrated that pupils could develop literacy skills in the target language without detracting from their achievement in oracy.

# Teachers talking

## Enhancing literacy skills through 'exploring language'

A Year 4 primary German teacher outlines a longer-term project called 'Exploring Language':

> If you want to get the most out of literacy work and language teaching, you've got to plan ahead. I introduced a longer-term project called 'Exploring Language' which I linked to the KAL strand of the Framework, but you obviously can't really separate KAL from literacy. Although we're learning German, I'm quite keen on language awareness issues in general, and comparing a number of languages really does get children thinking about how language works. This particular part of the project was called 'Comparing and Contrasting' and I introduced both the days of the week and the months of the year in German and French. We linked it to birthdays and other important dates like Christmas, school holidays and the introduction of the Euro. In small groups, pupils looked really closely at spellings, and practised the pronunciation of words. I did a lot of oral work first to ensure that their pronunciation was pretty good as I didn't want to confuse them with the written words, and their different sounds. Each group had to compare and contrast firstly the written word, and write their conclusions clearly and precisely in English. They then did the same with the spoken word. We had a whole-group brainstorm on key similarities and differences, and designed a poster for our display (Figure 4.1). It worked really well, it gave them all something to get their teeth into, and there was something in the activity that all pupils

Knowledge about Language: Comparing and Contrasting

Similarities and Differences – Ähnlichkeiten und Unterschiede – Ressemblances et Différences

The Months of the Year – Les mois de l'année – die Monate des Jahres

| English | français | Deutsch |
| --- | --- | --- |
| January | janvier | Januar |
| February | février | February |
| March | mars | März |
| April | avril | April |
| May | mai | Mai |
| June | juin | Juni |
| July | juillet | Juli |
| August | août | August |
| September | septembre | September |
| October | octobre | Oktober |
| November | novembre | November |
| December | décembre | Dezember |

**Figure 4.1**  Enhancing literacy skills through exploring language

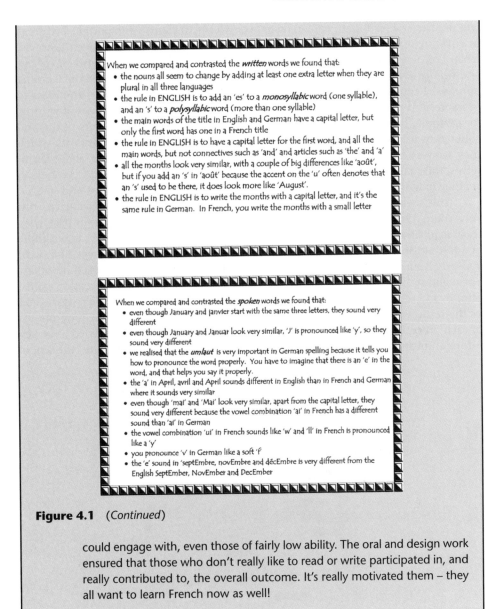

When we compared and contrasted the *written* words we found that:
- the nouns all seem to change by adding at least one extra letter when they are plural in all three languages
- the rule in ENGLISH is to add an 'es' to a *monosyllabic* word (one syllable), and an 's' to a *polysyllabic* word (more than one syllable)
- the main words of the title in English and German have a capital letter, but only the first word has one in a French title
- the rule in ENGLISH is to have a capital letter for the first word, and all the main words, but not connectives such as 'and' and articles such as 'the' and 'a'
- all the months look very similar, with a couple of big differences like 'août', but if you add an 's' in 'août' because the accent on the 'u' often denotes that an 's' used to be there, it does look more like 'August'.
- the rule in ENGLISH is to write the months with a capital letter, and it's the same rule in German. In French, you write the months with a small letter

When we compared and contrasted the *spoken* words we found that:
- even though January and janvier start with the same three letters, they sound very different
- even though January and Januar look very similar, 'J' is pronounced like 'y', so they sound very different
- we realised that the *umlaut* is very important in German spelling because it tells you how to pronounce the word properly. You have to imagine that there is an 'e' in the word, and that helps you say it properly.
- the 'a' in April, avril and April sounds different in English than in French and German where it sounds very similar
- even though 'mai' and 'Mai' look very similar, apart from the capital letter, they sound very different because the vowel combination 'ai' in French has a different sound than 'ai' in German
- the vowel combination 'ui' in French sounds like 'w' and 'll' in French is pronounced like a 'y'
- you pronounce 'v' in German like a soft 'f'
- the 'e' sound in 'septEmbre, novEmbre and décEmbre is very different from the English SeptEmber, NovEmber and DecEmber

**Figure 4.1**  (*Continued*)

could engage with, even those of fairly low ability. The oral and design work ensured that those who don't really like to read or write participated in, and really contributed to, the overall outcome. It's really motivated them – they all want to learn French now as well!

The teacher is careful to point out that the children need guidance in making the phoneme–grapheme correspondence and so much of this depends on the ability to make the connection and thus to be able to read. Reading is a rather neglected skill in languages and yet reading provides support for speaking and writing and an opportunity for creativity and extended learning. Interestingly, the children in the activities described are developing fully blended skills as they speak, listen to and read words and phrases as a lead-up to copying words down into a chart, an important first stage in enabling learners to write items of their own. A key point to remember, however, when you work on writing in the target language is to distinguish between *copying* and *writing*. Primary languages practitioners do need to be careful about the learning purpose of copying, and how too much can quickly demotivate learners and cease to promote active learning. Younger children are being taught the mechanics of writing, for example, how to hold a pen correctly, how to form individual letters neatly and coherently, how to write from left to right, and copying is thus something with which they are very familiar. Gradually they move on to creating longer texts, about themselves, their families, their interests, or recreating stories they have heard. As they do so, they practise spelling, punctuation, sentence and paragraph structure, and so on.

This sequence can be meaningfully modelled in the target language, even with very young children, provided the copying and/or writing activities keep pace with their acquisition of writing skills in their first language. Figure 4.2 shows an example of a KS1 writing activity. The teacher focused initially on building conversation, with a weekly homework practising copying, then identifying sentences worked on orally. Throughout the term, pupils took part in 'memory quizzes' to practise recreating words, phrases and sentences from memory, in order to move away from copying. At the end of the term, French was combined with art and photography as pupils took photos of each other, then designed their own poster, writing what they considered to be key information about themselves. They then created a whole-school display for the school

**Figure 4.2** Example of a KS1 literacy project: 'Moi'

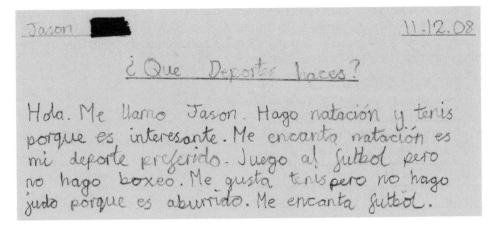

Jason ▇                                                    11·12·08

¿ Que Deportes haces?

Hola. Me llamo Jason. Hago natación y tenis porque es interesante. Me encanta natación es mi deporte preferido. Juego al futbol pero no hago boxeo. Me gusta tenis pero no hago judo porque es aburrido. Me encanta futbol.

**Figure 4.3** Individual literacy work based on whole-group learning, and small-group reinforcement

reception area. In this way, the teacher blended elements of the kinds of activities they were doing in the literacy hour with the core teaching and learning activities in French.

Enhancing pupils' meta-linguistic skills, and providing them with opportunity to use their developing awareness of language, comparing English with the target language, can be done very effectively through well-planned writing activities. Figure 4.3 shows an example of how a Year 6 group, having worked on the topic orally as a whole-group, then in smaller groups, begin in individual work to create more complex sentences in writing, and to express opinions about their favourite sports. The activity also gives pupils an opportunity to reflect on what they are learning, what they have learnt, and where they might need more support. The lesson included interlinked objectives:

- talking about favourite sports;
- comparing popular sports in England and Spain;
- using connectives in Spanish;
- recapping adjectives and gender agreement;
- expressing preferences, and giving reasons why.

## Strategies for developing oracy skills

Encouraging pupils to listen carefully, and to respond appropriately, is a core element of a teacher's activity. The classroom environment offers continuous opportunity for children to develop skills which enable them to understand and process the information they are receiving, and practitioners need to structure their own language in a way that allows pupils to access its meaning, both in English and the target language. Attention to appropriate voice modulation and clear and precise diction is necessary to ensure that pupils receive *de facto* a good model of speech, and are able to distinguish individual words from a series of sounds. Using mime, gesture, facial expression, eye contact, visual aids and realia all support comprehension in listening. As pupils listen to the target language, they can be encouraged to:

- listen for cognates;
- listen for individual, specified words;
- listen for *overall* meaning;
- infer meaning from context.

More challenging work would include:

- predict what might happen next;
- write in note form what is happening;
- summarize either verbally or in note form what has happened.

It is also important to encourage pupils to think positively and concentrate on what they *do* know, rather than worry about what they *don't* know. Including an appropriate number of unknown words in any listening activity or quiz is an effective strategy for developing listening skills, and building vocabulary, but too many unknowns will confuse and demotivate many young language learners.

There are several issues to note when you create a listening activity:

- the context must be linked to current learning;
- plan pre- and post-listening activities carefully;
- think carefully about the amount of time the activity will take, and what is reasonable in terms of pupil engagement with a single activity;
- how you will support less able learners (for example, if you have a pre-recorded dialogue, how many times will you play it?);
- how you will challenge more able learners (for example, including unknown or lesser known words).

Dictation is a useful listening activity in the primary languages classroom, and can enhance both oracy and literacy skills. It provides pupils with further support in relating the spoken to the written word and an opportunity to practise neat writing, punctuation, spelling and listening carefully simultaneously. As such, it is an example of a richly blended learning activity. Box 4.1 provides an example of a Year 5 Italian dictation, and related oracy/literacy activities.

---

**Box 4.1  Enhancing literacy and oracy skills through Italian dictation**

1   Ciao Gianna! (*punto esclamativo*)
2   Buonasera Mimo! (*punto esclamativo*)
3   Come stai Gianna? (*punto interrogativo*)
4   Sto bene, (*virgola*) grazie. (*punto*)

5   Arrivederci Mimo! (*punto esclamativo*)
6   A presto Gianna! (*punto esclamativo*)

- Use dictation as a means of enhancing listening skills, working on spelling and pronunciation; compare with English.
- To differentiate, think about length of text, speed at which you're dictating and the range of words you use – include some completely unknown words for more able children to encourage them to deconstruct sound, and reproduce it in written form – as the less able pupils become more familiar and comfortable with the language, include an unknown word in their dictation too.
- You can also leave out punctuation, asking pupils to add it as an additional activity – or use incorrect punctuation, asking pupils to identify errors, and correct them.
- As you read, think about diction – speak very clearly and precisely.
- Pupils can prepare small dictations for each other – this works well for writing, reading, speaking, pronunciation and presentation.
- Carousel activities enable you to include differentiated dictations in your lesson.
- Think about the language you use – try 'hand and ear quiz' rather than 'dictation' – can your hand write what your ear hears?
- Begin to draw up a grammar glossary in the TL – make it bilingual to reinforce knowledge of punctuation in English – remember to discuss function as well as meaning.
- Pupils can either come up to write short phrases on the board, or mark their own/ each other's work according to a model.

Listening to the teacher or a tape or other medium provides a model of speaking and an opportunity for the pupils to reproduce the kind of language they hear and even more importantly, to produce new variations of their own. Since listening and speaking blend naturally as in authentic 'speech acts', the teacher can exploit listening material for subsequent speaking practice, drawing on key vocabulary and expressions that the teacher wishes to practise and incorporating language items of the pupils' choice. Since it is important to let children create their own speaking texts, it will be equally important to monitor the quality of the children's utterances and to adopt a suitable attitude and approach to error correction.

## An approach to error

The primary languages classroom we are advocating encourages children to try out language and to take risks. We do not want children to be afraid to speak and not to wait until they think they have the perfect response. One outcome of this will be that children will make mistakes and that their language output will contain errors. It is important for teachers to distinguish between mistakes (temporary 'blips' that the pupils can be helped to recognize for themselves) and errors that reflect the learners' level of interlanguage, i.e. their current state of linguistic knowledge. In such cases, the most natural strategy is for the teacher to find other pupils or another teacher who may be in the room to model the correct response and provide an opportunity for pupils to hear, practise and internalize the correct response. The teacher can also model the correct response and then do whole class drill and practice. This kind of drilling allows all children to participate and can be made great fun by, for example, using different voices or rapping/singing. We are especially keen to encourage children to think about error for themselves and to learn to diagnose error with, for example, learning partners (see Chapter 5), even to anticipate likely errors. In this way children develop as strategic learners and error is seen as a rich source of learning. Beaton (1990) reported from his observations that most teachers appear to gear their strategies towards the pupil involved and not at the error, and that relationships with pupils was crucial in engendering a trusting atmosphere. It is, however, important that teachers collect error data and reflect on these in their lesson planning for the next stage.

## Pupil performance of language

We have noted that primary pupils are generally extremely enthusiastic about performing in front of their peers in the target language, and this is one of the key differences in pupil engagement with language learning between KS2 and KS3. The most successful lessons we observed always included opportunity for pupils to 'show' what they can do, and as they show and perform, they are simultaneously embedding language, and enhancing their oracy skills, particularly those in speaking, in a very proactive way, and supporting other pupils' learning. Figure 4.4 shows two pupils reading out their written texts on their favourite sports. The focus of the lesson is enhancing literacy (using connectives in Spanish to build compound sentences and to express opinions) with related oracy objectives of speaking to an audience and sound pronunciation.

## Presenting and practising new language

Presenting new language, and providing ongoing opportunities for pupils to practise it, revisit it and use it, are central to primary languages practice. Pupils will not embed language unless they have encountered it, processed it and had occasion to use it in different contexts over a significant period of time. It is in this way that pupils encounter and experiment with the grammatical structures of the language, compare them to their growing understanding of English grammatical structures, begin to make assumptions and choices, and test their own hypotheses about how language may work. Practitioners do need to be creative with language, and avoid always using specific language in specific contexts as this leads to pupils only being able to respond in a fixed way to a fixed prompt – we noted many examples of pupils being unable to process meaning when asked questions not framed in the way they normally heard from their teacher. For example, when asked 'Tu t'appelles comment?' by a visitor, pupils did not understand, as for two years they had heard only 'Comment t'appelles-tu?' and had not

**Figure 4.4**  Pupils perform to their peers in a literacy- and oracy-linked Spanish lesson

been encouraged to develop skills which would allow them to extract meaning from individual words, and to repackage those meanings to decode what was being said in a different way, even though the context remained the same.

At the presentation and practice stage, it is important that you speak clearly and model sound pronunciation. Using flashcards with pictures, mime, gesture or realia (such as classroom objects), say each word, getting pupils to repeat it. They will need to hear and repeat (both the word and the mime where appropriate) several times. Use a variety of question and answer (Q&A) techniques such as yes/no or true/false questions to give pupils a chance to begin to commit the words to their short-term memory.

There are certain key principles to bear in mind when presenting and practising new language that include:

- identifying the appropriate grammar and vocabulary for the particular activity, and recognising patterns related to prior learning;
- keeping the amount of new language manageable, and practising it adequately in different ways, looping backwards and forwards;
- ensuring the input is relevant to the age range and relates to real-life activities e.g. playing, doing sports;
- providing multi-sensory support with flashcards, mime, gesture, pictures, real objects (realia) and noises;
- moving on fairly speedily (15 minutes initial practice is ample) to giving pupils opportunities to use the new language;

- providing challenge with some difficult to guess words and tricky pronunciation;
- splitting longer words and phrases into syllables/phonemes and conducting pupils as with an orchestra as they learn the pronunciation;
- using an effective three-stage questioning technique (recognition, choice of response, open question), directed variously at whole class, groups, pairs and individuals;
- accepting both short and long responses to questions, but encouraging elaboration so as not to get 'stuck' at word level;
- rehearsing the pupils in question making and asking so that they can ask questions of each other;
- responding to error and reinforcing correct responses positively and with tact (e.g. whisper to a pupil needing support) and humour;
- finding ways to revisit the same material such as games and quizzes to consolidate learning at later stages;
- BUT avoiding presenting the written forms at this stage not just to avoid poor pronunciation but pupil reliance on the written word.

## Teacher and pupil language

Each lesson should comprise discrete categories of language:

- *teacher language* – the language that you will use to *teach* and the language you intend the pupils to *learn*;
- *pupil language* – the language the pupils will learn, and the language they might use to process learning.

As you begin to move away from a dependence on English, planning in advance how to simplify the target language in order to make it accessible to all learners as the language of instruction, is very important. Ofsted (2008) raised this point in their recent report, finding that trainees

> were not always clear about which key items of language they wanted pupils to learn or which skills they were emphasizing. The weakest planning risked pupils acquiring incorrect language forms or poor pronunciation. Many . . . did not plan in sufficient detail how to use the foreign language in lessons. While the very best trainees used the foreign language for all or most elements of the lesson, and planned carefully which items of language they would use and how they would develop them, many did not script their lessons in this way.
> (2008: 12)

Seeking to identify successful strategies in the primary languages classroom, they commented that the best lessons were those in which carefully planned use of the target language were the most effective:

The trainee used French for most of the lesson. She had a number of strategies to help pupils understand her, including repetition and mime, and asking pupils to translate the important elements of what she had said for the rest of the class. The lesson's progress was well supported by a very detailed lesson plan that showed the language to be taught and gave a timescale for each activity. For some parts of the lesson, the explanations were scripted in full. The trainee seemed to be able to keep spinning several plates at once, she was so well prepared. She knew the pupils well, praised them and recorded the merit points she awarded. Pupils made excellent progress.

(2008: 12)

Trainees we spoke to reported that where they didn't plan their own language in advance, they got confused, made errors in the target language and often resorted to English because pupils were unable to understand what they meant. One trainee commented:

## Trainees talking

Behaviour management in the target language was difficult at first, because I felt that pupils couldn't understand what I was saying. One day I was telling a pupil not to keep leaning back in his chair because it's dangerous and he could break his back, and I kept having to pause because the German grammar was quite complex. I lost the momentum, and in the end had to tell him off in English. When I discussed this back at Uni, my tutor said, 'Why didn't you just use a stern look, a raised finger, and say "Nein" in a fairly forceful voice – he'd get the message, you don't have to tell him off – he knows what he's doing is wrong and dangerous.' That made me realize that effective communication isn't about fluent German, it's about general teacher strategies, such as the stern look, and about choosing the key words that will get a message across – in this case 'Nein!'

Pupil language is also central to effective learning. As we see below, there are a number of useful strategies for promoting a generally target language-rich environment, but each lesson will contain *core learning content*, which may focus on both language, i.e. vocabulary and a particular grammar point, enabling learners to create sentences and phrases of their own. So for example, if you are working on animals, consider how many it is reasonable to introduce in different year groups at any one time. Six may be suitable for Year 3, while 8–10 may be more suitable for Year 6. Now think about *related learning content* – this is the language that pupils will use to actually contextualize the animals, and to begin to embed these units of vocabulary. For example, in French, this might be talking about domestic pets (as-tu un chien? Quel est ton animal préféré?) leading to a whole-class survey about domestic pets. What practitioners must avoid is simply teaching pupils banks of vocabulary, without giving them an opportunity to do something *with* the vocabulary. Creating a relevant and authentic context to practise and use language is absolutely key to effective learning. Thus, *embedding* language is a third stage in learning, after practice and production.

## Creating opportunities for communication in the target language in the classroom

As we discussed in Chapter 2, primary practitioners need to develop an adequate level of competence in the target language in order to provide a meaningful language learning experience for pupils. Many teachers we have spoken to expressed concern that their skills were insufficient to allow them to converse throughout an entire lesson in the target language. Beginning languages practitioners, however, should understand that complex language is not necessary, and indeed can create a barrier to learning – where teacher language is not accessible to learners, then they simply will not learn. As languages practitioners though, we do have a responsibility to maximize opportunities for children to be exposed to language – we have to remember that even where languages are formally timetabled, in the primary phase this is unlikely to exceed an hour a week, with many other lessons, events and weekends and holidays in between. This situation replicates a long-standing debate in secondary languages, where it has been argued that significant attainment in language learning is compromised by the relatively little exposure to language that pupils actually have – Hawkins described this as akin to 'gardening in a gale', where the seeds sown during the languages lesson would simply be swept away by the 'gale' of English that would envelop them as soon as the lesson was over. Macrory (2008: 107) makes a valid point when she warns that even 'sincere attempts' in the primary languages classroom 'may suffer from the pressure of covering the syllabus in a limited amount of time and thus may even be seen as tokenistic'. We would also argue that systematic use of the target language is a key component of inclusive practice in the primary languages classroom, creating a 'level-playing field' where, as discussed above, the main language of instruction, as well as curricular content, is equally new to all pupils. Practitioners should avoid the habit of using the target language then immediately repeating it in English, as many children become overly dependent on the English, and can 'tune out' of the target language. While we would advocate 'judicious' use of English, for example, when explaining the lesson objectives, we would argue that where there is not concerted effort to encourage pupils to listen, respond to and speak the target language as often as possible, thereby ensuring a frequency and continuity of exposure to it, and production of it, it is doubtful that any longer-term embedding of language is possible.

There are a number of strategies that can be used to promote both teacher and pupil use of the target language. These include:

- familiar classroom language for teacher and pupils (e.g. Wer ist fertig?, Puis-je aller aux toilettes?, Haben Sie einen Bleistift?);
- classroom instructions;
- classroom behaviour;
- greetings in and outside the classroom;
- conversational gambits in and outside the classroom such as asking the time;

- day, date, timetable on the whiteboard/IWB;
- verbal instructions for classroom activities and written instructions for work-sheets – decreasing the amount of English that may be used at the beginning of a languages programme as children become more familiar with the target language;
- introduce a 10- or 15-minute target language 'challenge', rewarding pupils who only speak or use the target language during that time which can be increased into whole-lesson challenges.

## Sequencing a primary languages lesson

As we discussed in Chapter 3, it is essential that you plan the sequence of the lesson, and the kinds of activities, very carefully. An effective sequence includes:

- starter activity: to warm up and to recap previous learning;
- sharing learning intentions: to give pupils a context for learning, so that they can understand its purpose;
- teaching and learning activities: core presentation, practice, production of language, with careful timing for each individual activity;
- plenary: bringing learning together and reflecting on learning; recap of learning intentions.

### Learning groups: individual, pair, small- and whole-group work

Varying the learning groupings within a languages lesson is a key strategy: whole-group starters allow both teacher and pupils to 'warm up', and are an effective way of recapping core content from previous lessons. If you are presenting new language, you may need to devote about 20 minutes to this, which means that whole-group work can sometimes last up to half an hour. We would suggest that a maximum of 15–20 minutes whole-group work is an effective start to a languages lesson, then moving on to smaller groups so that pupils can focus on language in a less 'busy' environment. Small group and pair work offer excellent opportunities for speaking and listening activities, and both shared and individual reading and writing activities give pupils chance to reflect on what they are learning, and to do something with it. This kind of activity also allows the teacher to move around the classroom, giving more personalized support to individual learners (see Figure 4.5).

## Embedding languages into school routines

As we saw in Chapter 1, primary languages are conceptualized as an integral element of the Primary National Strategy, and thus children's learning. If languages are to become part of the fabric of the primary experience, it is essential that they are embedded into school routines. This raises awareness of languages among governors, staff, parents and pupils, and simultaneously enhances their status.

**Figure 4.5**   Personalized support in small-group literacy work in a Year 6 Spanish class

## Teachers talking

### Embedding languages into school routines

A teacher talks about her approach to embedding French into school routines:

> I felt very strongly that in order to gain any mastery at all in French, pupils need to be exposed to it, and given opportunity to practise it, on a far more frequent and structured basis. I think it's really important to engage with grammar in both English and French as they actually support each other, and give pupils a chance to make their own sentences. My big success I felt was having French included on the school homework timetable [Figure 4.6], and we saw a surge of interest on the part of parents and older siblings, who were often called on not only to help, but to listen and observe. I use the homework as a reinforcement opportunity, and focus mainly on reading skills. Writing is somewhat challenging because really it's essentially just copying early on, and while copying has its value, I'm not convinced that endless copying of sentences is particularly fruitful. I keep homework quite simple,

**Figure 4.6** Example of reading homework

though not too simple – pupils have to work a lot of things out for themselves, but as time goes on, I'm beginning to set more challenging things, such as fact-finding and ICT presentations. Even those pupils with very poor reading skills in English, can engage with those activities, and it's encouraging them to sit down quietly for 10–15 minutes, which is generally manageable, and work with language.

I also sent out an invitation to families to join us in an after-school lesson, and that worked very well. I prepared certificates for the pupils, and used the session to award them for hard work and good learning. Another successful project was the reception area display I did with my class – I took a photo of each pupil, and we created short dialogues about ourselves, using language and conversation learned over a term, then we wrote them on card, decorated the card, and then inserted the JPEGs of each pupil onto their card – the display created a huge buzz around the school. I taught the days, months and numbers quite quickly, as well as school subjects, and now the date and the day's timetable is always written on the board in French, every morning – the pupils take it in turns to do that. All our greetings, both in and outside the classroom, are in French only! I've also introduced a 5-minute 'sans anglais' session every day, on top of our weekly timetabled lesson, where pupils get a merit if they only communicate with me and each other in French – they see that as a really fun challenge, and I'll probably increase it to ten minutes. Once a term we also perform a French assembly. It's really important that teachers identify opportunities for including the language in everyday activities, and to raise awareness of it throughout the school, and at home.

## A holistic approach to learning in the primary languages classroom

We can also work on multi-curricular targets within the primary languages classroom, and think beyond a simple pairing of the target language and developing reading skills for example. Figure 4.7 shows an example of what the primary Italian teacher calls a *holistic view* of learning – in this worksheet, she is addressing pattern recognition, non-verbal reasoning, numeracy skills, thinking skills, reading skills and Italian.

## Supporting learning through classroom and school display

Both classroom and school display need to be planned over the longer term if they are to support learning effectively. McLachlan (2009a: 111) comments:

> Classroom and school displays are an important learning tool, not only in terms of language learning, but also for working on literacy, presentation and creative skills. I'd recommend that pupils create as much of the . . . display material as possible, blending geographical, cultural and language elements. Some display work should be created on the computer, to provide opportunities to hone graphic design and general IT skills, but do encourage pupils to create art work from other materials too. Commercial language posters can work well, but do avoid putting up those dealing with aspects of French that pupils haven't covered yet as this can often affect pronunciation quite negatively, and doesn't actually mean anything to the pupils. To be effective, display has to support learning, not just look nice and, by creating much of the display themselves, pupils not only contribute to their own learning process, but also learn to take responsibility for, and pride in, their shared learning environment.

A well-thought out display should grow organically, celebrating children's achievement across the school year. A primary languages display is most effective when it is used by teachers and pupils as both a learning support tool and a discrete learning outcome *per se*. Thus, as McLachlan (2009a) points out, you should avoid using display as a merely decorative tool, as this soon becomes literally part of the wallpaper. An

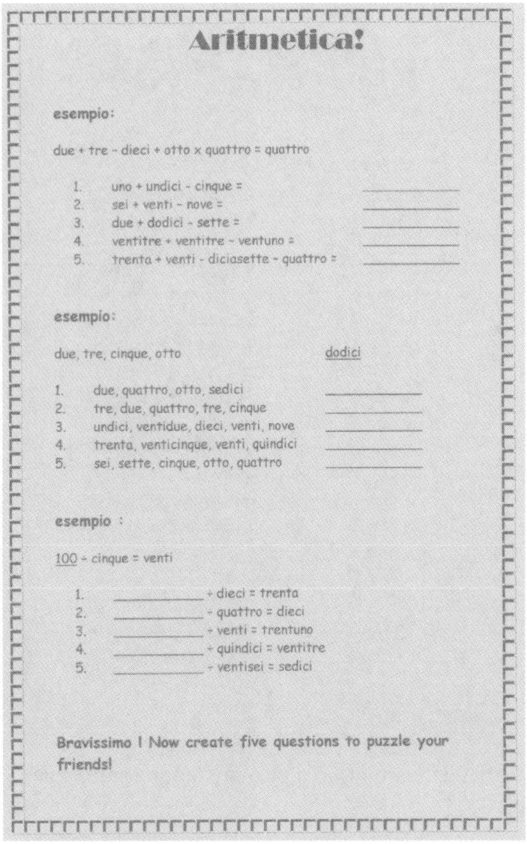

**Aritmetica!**

esempio:

due + tre – dieci + otto x quattro = quattro

1.   uno + undici – cinque =            _____
2.   sei + venti – nove =               _____
3.   due + dodici - sette =             _____
4.   ventitre + ventitre - ventuno =    _____
5.   trenta + venti - diciasette + quattro =  _____

esempio:

due, tre, cinque, otto                    dodici

1.   due, quattro, otto, sedici           _____
2.   tre, due, quattro, tre, cinque        _____
3.   undici, ventidue, dieci, venti, nove  _____
4.   trenta, venticinque, venti, quindici  _____
5.   sei, sette, cinque, otto, quattro     _____

esempio :

100 ÷ cinque = venti

1.   _____ + dieci = trenta
2.   _____ + quattro = dieci
3.   _____ + venti = trentuno
4.   _____ + quindici = ventitre
5.   _____ + ventisei = sedici

Bravissimo ! Now create five questions to puzzle your friends!

**Figure 4.7**   A holistic view of learning in the primary languages classroom

effectively planned display also creates an environment within which the target language is seen as an integral feature, and a focus on both cross-curricular learning and cultural exploration will enable you to embed languages into the life of the classroom, and to promote and confirm explicit learning links. Figure 4.8 is an example of a Year 3 poster designed in small group work to practise IT skills (page border, choice of font and centring text in Word), addition and French spelling. Related activities included a series of posters outlining the times tables in French, which were added to the display over the school year.

## Inclusive practice in the primary languages classroom

We have found that many of the strategies employed by practitioners to support pupils with lower levels of ability in literacy work can be effectively transferred to the

**Figure 4.8**   Cross-curricular learning in a primary languages display

primary languages classroom to support not only those children, but also those for whom English is a second, or additional language.

Evidence we have gathered suggests three key points:

1   Standard strategies that teachers employ to support the development of literacy and oracy in English pupils with lower-level skills work equally well to support all learners, as well as EAL pupils, in the primary languages classroom.

2   EAL pupils are in a continuous process of language learning, and thus learning the target language poses few, if any, problems or anxieties for them, providing the strategies employed by the teacher do not depend solely on native-speaker competence in English. The languages classroom becomes an 'even-playing field', where both the predominant language of instruction and the curriculum content (that is, the target language) are new to all pupils.

3   Pupils of a generally lower ability, who may underperform in other curriculum areas, gain in overall confidence in the languages classroom

where the focus is on active participation, and where all pupils are new to the language. Where robust support structures are in place, even when more competent linguists begin to move forward more quickly, less able learners will continue to engage with enthusiasm in the learning process.

Support strategies include:

- Focus on practical learning activities that require active participation, allowing pupils to watch, listen to, and be supported by, other children.
- Introduce a seating plan that groups children of varying abilities together, ensuring that EAL pupils are grouped evenly among those with English as a first language.
- Facilitate more personalized learning by designing small-group activities differentiated across levels of English language competence which will allow you opportunity to target specific groupings.
- Increase the use of visual prompts, aids and images in learning resources.
- Ensure that any written materials are clearly set out, with a reasonable amount of text, always giving an example that pupils can refer to as an additional support.
- Involve EAL pupils in the design of multilingual classroom language, routines and labels such as classroom objects, instructions, dates, timetables.
- Encourage the whole class to learn greetings and other common classroom language in the EAL pupils' first language – this will also actively include and involve the EAL pupils in the process.
- Ensure that concepts and forms being taught in the target language are systematically compared with English, as this not only contributes to the development of skills in English, but provides a familiar and non-threatening context for pupils to work in.
- An emphasis on prior knowledge, and continuous recapping will serve to embed language more effectively. Primary languages practitioners must avoid confusing 'what has been taught' with 'what has been learnt'.
- Focus on providing opportunities for children to develop as independent learners.

In the context of EAL learners, key points for the teacher to be aware of when designing support strategies are:

- in common with all pupils, EAL pupils will come from a variety of backgrounds, with varying degrees of exposure to spoken or written English;
- EAL pupils will have varying levels of general ability, and literacy/oracy skills in their first language.

Thus, an understanding of each child's previous experience of education is central to understanding how to offer differentiated support. Such experiences, Wood asserts, give 'grounds for optimism that ... children do have the potential, given appropriate experience, to overcome problems' (1998: 24).

## Effective teaching and learning in the primary languages classroom: some key points to consider

- Children learn at different paces and in different ways.
- The amount of new language we introduce has to be considered carefully – too much, and the pupils will get confused, too little and we are not challenging them sufficiently.
- It's easy to embed four-skill work from the very beginning of a primary language programme.
- Learners need lots of opportunity to practise new language.
- Recapping is a key element of language lessons.
- Some learners need to see the written word before they can fully process the spoken word – work on pronunciation a little first, then allow pupils to see the written word.
- Teach the numbers as quickly as you can – use for lots of numeracy activities, e.g. times tables, tens and units, general arithmetic – pupils can manage complex calculations in the target language and it's a fantastic way to work on both language and numeracy, particularly 'mental maths'.
- Ditto the alphabet – working on spelling in the target language enhances generic literacy skills and also enables pupils to engage with reading and writing in a more structured way – remember to progress from word to sentence to text – never underestimate your pupils' ability to rise to a challenge – making the challenge reasonable and achievable is the teacher's challenge!
- Building conversation – use topics they'll have something to talk about – age, where they live – and link this with wider exploration of environment, leading to France/Germany, etc. – be sensitive when it comes to families – make sure no-one's just died or got divorced, etc.
- We have to make language *relevant* – don't just teach colours for the sake of it – link it with world flags, or flags of French-/German-speaking countries, colours of the rainbow, favourite clothes or football strips – this links very nicely with other areas of the curriculum.
- Use songs, rhymes, poems, stories to motivate learners, and to provide a familiar learning framework.
- Develop meta-linguistic awareness, and relate the target language explicitly to English.

## Conclusion

This chapter has painted a portrait of a languages classroom that offers rich and varied learning opportunities that mesh with children's whole language and general development. Underpinned by key principles of relating to how individual children learn best and how teachers can make use of their own particular skills, a picture of structured cross-curricular teaching and learning, creating a *symbiosis* in learning, and a focus on language structures with clearly defined links to English, is beginning to emerge as effective and fruitful practice in primary languages.

# 5 Monitoring, assessing and recording progress in primary languages

## An AfL approach to primary languages

This chapter discusses how to:

- embed assessment into your planning and teaching
- adopt an AfL approach to language teaching and learning
- consider approaches to assessing progress in language learning at KS2.

## Introduction

There is a clear rationale for establishing a framework of systematic assessment in the primary languages classroom, based on the principle of continuous feedback: monitoring and evaluating pupil learning informs effective planning and ensures progression in learning, and allows both teachers and learners to understand the learning process, and to set reasonable and appropriate targets, engaging learners themselves directly in the process. Learners are involved directly in the process, and are encouraged to be aware of, and define, their achievements, to set personal learning goals, and to understand and plan what they need to do to move forward in their learning. Creating an Assessment for Learning (AfL)-rich languages classroom where assessment is integrated into teaching and learning, where teaching and learning activities are formative, simultaneously providing a template for progression, promotes a classroom community of learning that is collaborative, purposive and reflective.

Rather than planning assessment as 'add-on' or extraneous to their developing pedagogy of teaching and learning, it is important that primary language teachers integrate assessment into their teaching. Teaching, learning and assessment form a triangle that provides the frame for language learning and serves as an integral mechanism for progression. The triangle is firmly located in an Assessment for Learning approach in which assessment becomes formative when it drives learning forward on the basis of feeding back. Assessment, no longer seen as inappropriate or a dampener on the fun of primary language learning, has become a key way to focus and progress learning and provides useful feedback for both teacher and learners. A carefully devised and practised assessment method can furnish ongoing data as well as summative 'snapshots' of what children know and are able to do, as well as where they may be experiencing difficulties. The latter comprises important data providing a benchmark for both progress and planning purposes, which enables teachers to modify their teaching in the light of feedback received. Assessment opportunities crucially provide feedback for pupils, giving them opportunities to become more aware of their own learning and to think of ways to progress. In 2008, Ofsted highlighted the widespread lack of structured and informed assessment in primary languages and reports that: 'Formal assessment in languages, as a relatively new subject of the primary curriculum, is generally underdeveloped ... Too many trainees kept no records of pupils' progress in languages' (2008: 14), and as we move towards entitlement provision, it is timely to reflect on the purposes and most effective means of assessment as in the activity below.

---

## Box 5.1  Assessment for Learning – definitions

> The term 'assessment' refers to all those activities undertaken by teachers, and by their students in assessing themselves, which provide information to be used as feedback to modify the teaching and learning activities in which they are engaged.
>
> (Black and Wiliam 1998)

Assessment for Learning involves:

> Gathering and interpreting evidence about students' learning; and learners and their teachers using that evidence to decode where students are in their learning, where they are going and how to take the next steps.
>
> (Black and Wiliam 1998)

Five key factors that improve learning through assessment:

- providing effective feedback to children;
- actively involving children in their own learning;
- adjusting teaching to take account of the results of assessment;
- recognizing the profound effect on motivation and self-esteem;
- considering the need for children to know how well they are doing and what they need to do to improve further.

(DfES 2004c)

---

## Activity

- Bearing in mind the definitions of AfL provided in Box 5.1, to what extent is assessment embedded into practice at your school?
- Does current assessment in Languages reflect the whole-school policy on assessment across the curriculum?

## Pupils talking

When assessment is essentially formative and approached in a natural way, a primary classroom holds little fear for pupils. They can see assessment as an integral part of their learning sequences, rather than approaching formal tests with anxiety or boredom, and viewing them as an interruption in the learning process. This is evident in the responses of Year 5 pupils learning in an AfL-rich classroom when questioned about fear and assessment in languages:

> No, because it is not a test about where you have to worry about getting all the answers right.

> You can think of something you did right, that's your star, and something you are stuck on and can work on it, that's your wish.

> Our assessment is not scary, it's not as though it is life-threatening, it's just a bit of fun that shows me what I am good at and tells Miss what I need to work on.

These confident statements reflect the children's understanding of assessment as one that is supportive, integrated into lessons, feedback-rich and forwardly orientated. This resonates with Black et al.'s assertion that assessment for learning 'is usually informal, embedded in all aspects of teaching and learning, and conducted by different teachers as part of their own diverse and individual teaching styles' (2003: 2). Assessment when incorporated into any normal classroom activity can promote learning 'if it provides information to be used as feedback by teachers, and by their students in assessing themselves and each other, to modify the teaching and learning activities in which they are engaged' (Black et al., 2003) This definition of the purpose of assessment shows that it works best with current and developing effective primary languages practice which recognizes the power of feedback for self-learning and progression.

## Activity

The influential pamphlet *Inside the Black Box* by Black and Wiliam (1998) summarized findings from a trawl of international research and has acted as a touchstone for many in the field of assessment. With reference to the five key factors outlined in Box 5.1, consider to what extent these factors are a feature of primary languages provision and reflect upon their impact on pupil learning.

# Assessment for Learning: putting it into practice

The ongoing 'Black Box' research has shown how pupils who experience consistent feedforward for learning derive many benefits in their learning and progress: interventions also increased test scores beyond predictions at secondary level. While we are not looking at advancing SATs scores at primary level, the 2008 Ofsted report asserted that the lack of progression is an issue, and it has been for some time (see for example, Galton et al. 1999, on the 'discontinuities' at the primary to secondary transition). An AfL approach provides a platform to enable pupils to progress and opportunities for teachers to utilize techniques that are consistent with good primary practice and assessment initiatives in the primary school. While the focus is on individual pupils taking responsibility for aspects of their own learning, collaboration is a key feature of this classroom. Group work is a means for pupils to practise taking responsibility for aspects of their own learning and to act as a resource for their peers.

What is of particular use from the repertoire of AfL techniques (see Jones and Coffey 2006) that have been identified as pertinent to and manageable for the development of an AfL culture of ongoing feedback are rich questions (with the associated practice of no hands-up), traffic-lighting or the thumb tool, two stars and a wish feedback, and regular and consistent use of peer and self-assessment, each of which we explore in turn.

## Rich questions

Our young learners are of course restricted to some extent by linguistic limitations and their maturational levels. There will inevitably be much practising at word and short sentence level in the primary languages classroom and simple questions to elicit basic language at this stage. An example of this would be:

> Teacher (with flashcard or soft toy): Was ist das?
>
> Pupil: Das ist ein Wellensittich.
>
> Teacher: Ja, sehr gut!

While very complex or open-ended questions may be beyond the linguistic scope of the primary languages learner, it should be possible to enable pupils to do the following:

- Respond individually to questions other than simple naming questions.
- Respond in pairs or groups to more complex questions.
- Use more question formats themselves.

Extending the previous simple budgie-naming Q/A and bearing the above points in mind, lead to the following in one classroom:

> Teacher: Dieser Wellensittich ist grün oder blau?
>
> Pupil: Blau.

*Teacher*: Ja, magst du den grünen Wellensittich oder den blauen Wellensittich?

*Pupil*: Der blauen (sic) Wellensittich.

*Teacher*: Warum? Warum magst du den blauen Wellensittich? (Points to descriptor options on IWB and flashcards on wall and waits a while.)

*Pupil*: Der blau (sic) Wellensittich ist schön.

*Teacher*: Und ihr? (to other pupils). Now tell your buzz partner which budgie you like and why. Sage deinem Arbeitspartner welchen Wellensittich du magst und warum.

Pupils then ask each other similar questions using other pets.

In this real extended Q&A sequence, the teacher has interestingly chosen to use the word 'Wellensittich' as a challenge to the pupils, one which they embraced enthusiastically. Where teachers feel such a long word would strike terror into the heart of pupils, then something easier like 'Vogel' or 'Goldfisch' could be substituted.

Within a trustful classroom atmosphere, there is no need always for 'hands up' (a habit that is well and truly instilled at primary school) as the expectation is that all pupils will have equal access to the teacher and the answer time, that all important 'wait time', to think out an answer. No hands up is another mark of trust that the teacher will not pounce like a lion in the bush but will, after time to think (one of those things that take a little practice to establish the optimal timing), ask any of the pupils for a response.

There is certainly scope in the primary languages classroom for extended questions; it is important to remember that this is not just about questions *per se* but about enhancing opportunities for pupil dialogue and richer feedback. To obtain this kind of feedback, there are techniques such as traffic-lighting and the thumb tool that can be used to good effect in primary language classrooms.

## Traffic lighting and the thumb tool

These are simple procedures whereby pupils can indicate their level of understanding of the input/task to the teacher. With traffic lights, pupils are given or, preferably make, a set of 'traffic lights'. We have seen a variety of these that include moving versions made out of cardboard, small football penalty-style bits of card in green, amber and red, coloured circles or table tennis balls on lollipop sticks and coloured soft toys. Children see these as motivating and find them easy to indicate 'got it' (green), 'not too sure' (amber) and 'don't understand' (red) when asked by the teacher whether they understand. The showing of the appropriate colour can be done discreetly by the child, and the display gives instant feedback to the teacher about the overall level of understanding and where support needs to be targeted.

**Figure 5.1**  Lollipop traffic lights

Some teachers prefer the thumb tool as they do not like the semiotics of the red and simply ask pupils for a show of either thumbs up, across or down, signifying the same levels of understanding as with the traffic lights. Pupils also can use traffic light stickers or highlighters against any record of work that they keep. Far from being a gimmick, such tools have an important role in giving immediate feedback to the teacher and inform about the next stage. Very importantly, for the pupils, these tools ensure opportunities to reflect individually on their learning and level of understanding.

## Two stars and a wish

With feedback being at the centre of an AfL approach, a very simple way in which to provide feedback to pupils is to use the 'two stars and a wish' format, two good features (two stars) and one area for development (a wish). It is a format that children, even very young ones given the simplicity of the frame, can be taught to use very effectively. Psychologically, pupils know that their teachers using two stars and a wish will focus their feedback on the positive yet indicate a way to improve in a less successful area. When teachers adopt this method, pupils know they will not be penalized or subject to negative comment, strange expressions or angry-looking red marks. One teacher who uses both self- and peer assessment with the two stars and a wish format, provides an example of the format:

---

## 'Two stars and a wish' self-assessment

Name: Ethan            Date:
Learning Intentions:

- I can use each of the 7 verbs correctly.
- I can change the verbs to match with 'Ich'.
- I can say whether I like doing something or not.
- ☼ I can use each of the 7 verbs correctly
- ☼ I can change the verbs to match with 'ich'
- ☻ I wish can do it quicker

## 'Two stars and a wish' peer assessment

of Ethan          by Ewan          Date:
Learning Intentions:

- He/she can use each of the 7 verbs correctly.
- He/she can change the verbs to match with 'Ich'.
- He/she can say whether they like doing something or not.
- ☼ he can use each of the verbs correctly
- ☼ he can change verbs
- ☻ princyation (sic) may need a bit of work

---

### Self-assessment and peer assessment

We discussed error correction in Chapter 4 and stressed that it needs to be done sensitively and constructively. The children themselves seem to do it very effectively (the above comments come from Yr 4 pupils, aged 8) and are very receptive to their peers' comments (Jones 2010). In the classroom learning community that we wish to promote, considerable responsibility for learning, then, is on the pupils as is the assessment of their own learning and, in the case of peer assessment, that of their peers. Here traffic lighting and 'two stars and a wish' provide useful mechanisms for self- and peer assessment. It needs to be pointed out that pupils need training and practice in these techniques and increasingly incorporated into lessons. Learning intentions and success criteria need to be shared with and understood by the pupils. The skills of self-assessment are best developed before peer assessment so that children develop a familiarity with the language of assessment, the appropriate comments and expression in their feedback. Once the children have practised and are confident, they assess very constructively, honestly and kindly towards their peers.

Peer assessment thus can provide friendly and critical feedback to children that they find comprehensible and acceptable. Pupils also report that they learn from their peers and get ideas from each other. Children need to be reassured that sharing knowledge is useful and nothing to do with 'copying' and that the languages classroom functions as a learning group. All these activities provide feedback that serves to move learning forwards through the identification of targets, the 'wishes'. There will ideally be a rich medley of targets from teachers, and pupils themselves, as in the following comments:

> I am learning that 'sac' is masculine so my = 'mon'.

> My target is to remember the newer and bigger words like Federmäppchen. It helps me to chant them especially if they've got more than one syllable, not like Buch and Heft which are fine.

> I want to be able to link topics together, like sewing them together.

> I only have one target, that's to pronounce the rrrrrs and things. I haven't told my teacher this target.

Feedback to the whole class as a result of the teacher 'noticing' what is going on with the learning during a lesson is also a valuable plenary exercise, for feedback should not be relegated to the end but acted upon as the need arises (Clarke 2001). Being attuned to progressing learning 'as and when' underscores an approach to assessment that articulates with inbuilt progression through the Attainment Targets (ATs), and incorporates the Languages Ladder construct of 'assess as you go'. The approach also ties in well with a portfolio style of pupil reflexivity and of recording ongoing achievement. We begin by referring to the ATs (for Key Stages 3 and 4 but levels 1–4 potentially applicable at primary level) and how these articulate with our suggested formative approach.

## Attainment Targets and AfL

The ATs provide an opportunity to plan assessment around the four skills as exemplified in the level descriptors. AT1 listening, level 2, for example, requires pupils to be able to 'show that they understand a range of familiar statements and questions (for example, everyday classroom language and instructions for setting tasks). They respond to a clear model of standard language, but may need items to be separated.' An assessment task might comprise groups of pupils being given simple oral instructions in the target language that would include some extended sentences to create a family of wooden spoons using bits of coloured felt and wool with felt tips. The teacher would specify certain features then leave the pupils to create their spoon folk. If the teacher also specified and had pre-practised, for example, the colours, numbers and phrases such as 'Je voudrais', 'Je n'aime pas' and 'Donne-moi ça', then the assessment task could become a task to assess AT2 speaking simultaneously. Undertaking this task, the pupils would certainly key into level 1 ('single words and short phrases') and some pupils might achieve level 2 ('they describe people ... they use set phrases ... meaning is clear'. Thus, in one challenging, interactive activity, the teacher could assess the pupils' understanding in AT1 and AT2, moving from group to group and/or undertaking focused assessment with one group and recording assessment data of the children in that group. At the appropriate age and stage, it is a short step to the creation of a reading task related to the spoon activity (AT3, reading, level 3, 'Pupils show that they understand short texts ... made up of familiar language') with abler pupils attempting to write a paragraph of description of the spoons (AT4, writing, level 4, 'Pupils write two or three short sentences on familiar topics').

Such multi-modal and blended skill assessment reflects real language use and provides opportunities for children to achieve their best in their own ways and at their own pace. The teacher can build up a profile of each pupil in individual AT columns with comments relating to task criteria, which would have transferable validity from teacher to teacher. One teacher used colour coding to indicate levels, thus providing a rainbow image of the pupils' achievement overall. The data give a clear indication of where pupils are and in which skill they need to improve. When pupils become involved in assessing their own progress with the ticking of simple 'can do' statements, relating to assessment criteria, for example, that resonate with the level descriptors, and when they can engage in meaningful constructive feedback in peer assessment, then assessment in the form of constant feedback can become a powerful tool for learning and one of which pupils can take some ownership as they create their own learning progression 'ladders'.

## Up the ladder: gathering assets

Laddering is a useful image of learning, for it captures the fact that learning is not in fact a simple linear progression as we gingerly negotiate the steps of the ladder that features stops and starts and involves the learner in repositioning, exploring, anchoring and making all manner of adaptations to and expanding known constructs. The concept is far from new and was written about by the late Brian Page in the 70s when he advocated a languages assessment system that mirrored the graded tests that are taken for musical instruments on an 'as and when' basis, and that was a herald of the graded objectives movement.

The Languages Ladder, the national recognition of achievement scheme for languages that is promoted by the DSFC and that runs alongside other assessment frameworks, is designed to be used flexibly, across any or all of the four skills, at any age, at any stage, in any context, in a wide range of languages. The Ladder enables progress to be captured separately in each of the four key language skills: speaking, listening, reading and writing. It is necessary to remember though that many language learners need a blend of all four skills in their language programme to access new language successfully, even if their progress within individual skills is not uniform.

Reflecting the assessment framework of the *Common European Framework* (CEF), 'a resource for assessment' (Council of Europe 2001, see Chapter 6), the levels are entirely positive in the form of 'can do' statements that go from the beginners' breakthrough level to mastery level. 'It is not just about school assessment but provides a portable support for lifelong learning' (2001: 2). The Languages Ladder is administered by *Asset Languages*. Formal assessment is possible in two ways: teacher assessment leading to an Asset Languages Grade Award Certificate – this can be in any skill, at any grade, and external assessment through Asset Languages, in any skill, at any grade. Each skill is tested separately, and there are a number of testing dates per year.

If you are considering using the Languages Ladder in your school, contact Asset Languages for information on how to register as an accredited centre: www.assetlanguages.co.uk. If we look at the levels of competence and what they mean in terms of equivalence, it can be seen that breakthrough provides the ideal and attainable level for primary pupils:

| | | |
|---|---|---|
| Breakthrough | Grades 1–3 | beginners |
| Preliminary | Grades 4–6 | lower GCSE |
| Intermediate | Grades 7–9 | higher GCSE |
| Advanced | Grades 10–12 | AS and A level |
| Proficiency | Grades 13–15 | UG ML |
| Mastery | Grades 16 & 17 | PG ML |

## The Languages Ladder in action

Assessment can take place at any stage on the basis of discussion between the teacher and the learner and when there is evidence to decide that the learner is ready; there is no prescription for a specific stage in learning. Assessment can be in any of the four skills as exemplified below:

### Progressing through the listening stage

Breakthrough (Grades 1, 2, 3)

1   I can understand a few familiar spoken words and phrases.
2   I can understand a range of familiar spoken phrases.
3   I can understand the main points from a short spoken passage made up of familiar language.

*On completing this stage*: you should be able to understand a basic range of everyday expressions relating to personal details and needs. You may need to listen several times to get the information you need, depending on how fast and clearly the speaker talks. You should have some understanding of a few simple grammatical structures and sentence patterns. You should be familiar with the sound system of the language. You should be aware of how to address people both formally and informally as appropriate.

As with all new initiatives, it takes time for teachers to adapt to the scheme and to interpret it for their own approach and then integrate it into their own practice. Views, as would be expected, are varied, with some teachers expressing diffidence and a lack of confidence and some feedback concerning children's anxiety about the testing. One teacher commented on the 'insecurity' of the NC levels

> because of the lack of precision regarding the definition of simple/complex/ long/short/familiar/unfamiliar and the range and weighting given to 'express- ing opinions'. Personally I feel that there has to be a link to content, e.g. amount of vocabulary/grammar/functions to make it meaningful. The Lan- guages Ladder is even less precise and seems to make the levels even 'easier' to achieve in the way I read them.

This clearly expresses a need for specific assessment targets to be set and the lack of specificity remains an issue for many teachers.

It is, however, the broad expectation that the Ladder is integrated into a school's primary languages assessment policy and in the following interview, one teacher, her- self acknowledging the lack of precision in some respects, outlines how this can be done:

---

## Teachers talking

### Using the Languages Ladder to assess pupil learning

Q: *Tell me how you actually operate the Ladder and how it fits into the normal scheme of your primary languages teaching.*

A: We have incorporated the tests into our scheme of work. Being able to adapt many of the tests makes this quite straightforward. We aim to do the internal grades 1–3 in Years 3, 4 and 5 and then the external assessments in Year 6. We offer all four skills.

Q: *What general assessment approach have you adopted?*

A: AfL. Some schools also choose to keep the Languages portfolio.

Q: *How well has the Ladder been working? What are its strengths and weaknesses?*

A: Generally it works well with the internal grades. The children can have further attempts if necessary and it is very low-key and light touch. External assessments often depend on specific vocabulary which may, or may not, have been covered. Speaking tests are time-consuming and require extra staff/rooms. Some of the picture tasks are quite tricky to use.

Q: *How do children feel about the ladder? Do they find it scary or just like another activity?*

A: Children are quite happy about it. They see the internal grades as just another activity. The external ones are much more formal but the children are quite happy about it.

---

Q: *How do you help prepare the children in your lessons?*

A: For the internal ones, we build up to the tests in our lessons. For the external ones, we prepare the speaking as far as possible – pictures for presentations, etc. following the guidelines from the teachers' handbook.

Q: *How do you record the children's progress?*

A: On the progress sheets supplied, copies of which go to the secondary schools.

The ladder then, as a flexible assessment scheme, can support formative assessment, and complement an AfL approach to language learning. With skilled and confident self- and peer assessment, pupils can develop learning strategies and the reflexive skills needed for portfolio style of assessing that can be incorporated into a scheme of work.

# What is the European Languages Portfolio (ELP)?

The ELP is a tool for reflection on and self-recording of achievement in language learning and increased intercultural understanding. It provides a teacher's tool for assessment and recording for the teacher. There are two portfolios: one for vocational learning, the other for language learners in the primary phase.

## How does it work?

- The Portfolio remains the property of the learner, regardless of context or learning environment.
- All learning, both formal and informal, is valued.
- Promotes lifelong learning.
- Promotes reflection and self-assessment.
- Linked to the Common European Framework of Reference for Languages: http://www.coe.int/t/dg4/linguistic/Source/Framework_EN.pdf
- *My Languages Portfolio* is the primary school version of the ELP, which pupils can also fill in online, on www.nacell.org.uk
- Is suitable for a wide range of European and community languages.

## What's in the primary version?

There are three main sections.

### 1 My Language Biography

The biography contains 'can do' statements for children to colour in and complete as they learn, creating a personal learning diary, and actively involving children in their own learning.

There are sections for listening, speaking, talking to someone, reading, writing and intercultural understanding.

### 2 My Dossier

Children collect and collate their own work as a record of their achievement and progress. The dossier encourages children to look after their work carefully, and to take pride in it.

### 3 My Languages Passport

The passport aims to provide an overview of the language(s) a child is learning, and can include both school and home input and experience. There is a self-assessment section which contains a summary of Council of Europe levels for each skill (Breakthrough, A1, Preliminary A2 and Intermediate B1). It also contains the first nine grades of the Languages Ladder. The ELP can be downloaded in full on: http://www.nacell.org.uk/resources/pub_cilt/portfolio.htm

The Council of Europe provides further information about the Portfolio in action: http://culture2.coe.int/portfolio

We suggest that the portfolio is a useful umbrella document that serves to focus the children on the totality of their work and range of skills required and it allows them to visualize and take pride as they reflect on progress, achievements and targets for the next stages.

## Records of learning and targets for learning

The primary languages teacher needs to create and sustain a record of learning progression for both internal reference but also as a means to inform the transition process: it is important to provide secondary colleagues with assessment data and records that they can build on. We think it is also important that pupils learn to keep a record of their learning, keeping feedback comments, any marks, targets, details of successes and learning ideas. We have seen samples of these, such as large format A4 scrap books that included worksheets and other handouts that served as an *aide-mémoire* for future reference, and small A5 booklets with mini-work sheets, tick lists and topic vocabularies.

In one Cheshire primary school, little home-made booklets made by the children them-selves contained learning targets, 'hot tips' for learning and snippets of cultural infor-mation that the children had found of personal interest, creating their own portfolio of learning that complements in some respect the ELP.

Such documentation will be a useful focus of discussion in the conversation about learning that needs to take place about learning between primary and secondary lan-guage teachers. In such a conversation, on which we elaborate in Chapter 7, teachers would have a useful record on which to build and progress learning and have grounds for committing themselves to do so.

## Teachers talking

Teachers discuss recording progress and assessment:

I've always felt that to make French something that the children took seriously I had to teach it – and they had to learn it – in the same way we work with every subject. Some colleagues felt that this would take the fun out of things, but I really do disagree with that – who says real learning can't be fun? What that meant in practice was that I had to develop strategies for both teacher and pupil self-assessment into the whole programme, in exactly the same way we do for maths, English and science. So as such, I wasn't creating anything new – I was embedding normal, and very effective, practice, into this new subject. I used the attainment targets because I felt they were easily understandable, and the Languages Ladder hadn't been fully developed. I'm happy with the attainment target descriptors, and so are the pupils – they've become part of our learning canon. I've heard that a lot of secondary teachers don't particularly like level descriptors because they are essentially fairly vague, but I do know that they work very well at KS2, and more importantly, the pupils have really got to grips with them, and taken them on board – they are always checking whereabouts they are, and if they can say their performance at a particular level is 'consistent' – lots of healthy debate about how to define and quantify 'consistent'!

I use three charts – one is my chart where I record pupil progress on a termly basis in all the four areas. Another thing I felt strongly about was including reading and writing activity in our French learning, and having them explicit on my chart does help me plan with all four skills in mind. I also include information on the assessment activities so that as a whole-school team, we can have some kind of consistency from year to year, and keep track of resources. I wanted to include some very simple sub-levels because it adds a level of healthy challenge for the pupils, and does give a little bit more information about the extent to which I – and the pupils – think they have really learnt how to do something. I add a couple of qualitative comments per pupil, and we do set targets together. I really like the chart, and would like all staff to use it – it would build up into a really sound record of achievement we could hand over at Year 7. (See Figure 5.2: French progress and attainment chart.)

Each pupil has a self-assessment chart which we have up on display – as we work through things, they can note where they think they are. They can do this at any time, but I do like to devote some targeted time to it as well – 15 minutes where we discuss as a group where we think we are, if we are hitting our targets, the kinds of things we might do to practise certain areas and so on. (See Figure 5.3: Pupil Self-assessment Chart.) I also adapted the level descriptors slightly, and those are on display too, for general reference. (See Fig 5.4 Les niveaux en français.) I think if we embed this into whole-school practice, we will capture attainment and set targets very effectively, and really focus pupils on their own learning – yes, it's serious, but it's fun!

Class _____     Term/Date_____

**Assessment Activities**
**AT1:** teacher observations - formative; fortnightly listening quiz; end of term listening competition
**AT2:** teacher observations – formative; structured/semi-structured role-play; conversation quiz (teacher-led)
**AT3:** classroom activities/quizzes (formative); short (differentiated) comprehension on familiar topic with questions in both English & Spanish
**AT4:** classroom activities/quizzes (formative); writing dialogue (role-play); writing short letter to penfriend 'Yo'
**Other:** short dictations to practise both listening and spelling; creative writing with emphasis on role-play/performance; display work

**Sub-levels:**
a = consistently achieved
b = frequently achieved
c = occasionally achieved

| Pupil Name | AT1: Listening & Responding | AT2: Speaking | AT3: Reading & responding | AT4: Writing | Teacher Comments | Targets for next term |
|---|---|---|---|---|---|---|
| | | | | | | |
| | | | | | | |
| | | | | | | |

**Figure 5.2** French progress and attainment chart

## Towards a languages assessment plan

It can be seen from these examples that assessment is often very single-skill focused, in order to provide a skill profile for each child and to avoid what is known in assessment

Mon progrès en français!

*Bonjour!*

Je m'appelle_____

| L'automne | Niveau | Mes Commentaires | Madame dit... |
|---|---|---|---|
| Ecouter | | | |
| Parler | | | |
| La lecture | | | |
| L'écriture | | | |

J'ai plusieurs exemples de mon travail dans mon portefeuille de compétences                                                            Oui/Non

| Le printemps | Niveau | Mes Commentaires | Madame dit... |
|---|---|---|---|
| Ecouter | | | |
| Parler | | | |
| La lecture | | | |
| L'écriture | | | |

J'ai plusieurs exemples de mon travail dans mon portefeuille de compétences                                                            Oui/Non

| L'été | Niveau | Mes Commentaires | Madame dit... |
|---|---|---|---|
| Ecouter | | | |
| Parler | | | |
| La lecture | | | |
| L'écriture | | | |

J'ai plusieurs exemples de mon travail dans mon portefeuille de compétences                                                            Oui/Non

*Au revoir!*

**Figure 5.3** Pupil self-assessment chart

discourse as 'muddied measurement'. However, we would like to emphasize the need for a more holistic assessment that would involve pupils in more natural multi-skill language-using assessment scenarios. An example of this is a Yr 6 class taking it in turns to do a role – play around a breakfast table in the classroom, with real breakfast items such as croissants, jam and hot chocolate brought in by the teacher for the children to consume. Each group, after a period of preparation, performs their little play and the others peer assess according to criteria drawn up by the whole class. The teacher then asks the groups to self-assess their learning and performance and to decide targets for improvement/extension. The teacher makes notes for herself in an assessment diary of

| | |
|---|---|
| **Niveau 1**<br><br>I can write or copy simple words or symbols correctly.<br>I can label items and select appropriate words to complete short phrases or sentences. | **Niveau 2**<br><br><br>I can write one or two short sentences, following a model, and fill in the words on a simple form. I can label items and write familiar short phrases correctly. When I write familiar words from memory, my spelling isn't always right, but it's very close. |
| **Niveau 3**<br>I can write a few short sentences, with some help, using expressions that I have already learnt. I can express personal responses.<br><br>I can write short phrases from memory and my spelling is easily understandable. | **Niveau 4**<br>I can write short texts on familiar topics, adapting language that I have already learnt. I use a lot of language that's now in my memory. I am beginning to use my knowledge of grammar to adapt and substitute individual words and set phrases. I am using dictionaries or glossaries to check words I have learnt and sometimes to find brand new ones. |

**Figure 5.4** Les niveaux en français: L'écriture (pupil self-assessment)

each group's strengths and weaknesses. The skills in such a scenario are blended as are the assessment and the learning. Such assessments would be a useful end of topic format and are very time-efficient in enabling the teacher to evaluate whole-class progression in learning. They also provide a summative record, for as Martin writes: 'summative assessment is retrospective: it looks back on what the child has achieved' (2008: 107).

In order to monitor progression, the languages teacher needs to have a languages assessment plan to fit with the whole-school assessment policy and to articulate with the whole-school approach to formative assessment. It is fairly straightforward to incorporate assessment opportunities into a scheme of work, linking the assessments to AT levels and skills drawn from the framework. Teachers can incorporate Ladder assessments into the overall plan, all the while maintaining some flexibility according to the needs and progress of their pupils. It is important that effective and transparent records be kept to sustain that cross-phase 'conversation about learning'.

## Conclusion: developing a 'learning group' culture

The languages classroom in which AfL is embedded successfully can be recognized by collaboration and openness and makes children feel secure and empowered as the encouraging teacher and supportive peers welcome the efforts of all. It is very inclusive culture in this respect (Clarke 2003). Such a classroom takes time to develop and teachers need the space and time to practise and experiment with the tools that AfL generates. An appropriate balance between collaborative and individual tasks needs to be found, respecting pupils' needs for their own quiet thinking moments, and for the recognition of their individual effort, in the very busy and dynamic MFL classroom. Incorporating too much group work into lessons or using too many individual tasks creates an imbalance; on this, it is a question of practice.

Assessment can be done in an informal way, opportunistically or 'on the fly', as well as in a planned structured way but the guiding principles are feedback and the development of the children's own learning resources for themselves as well as being a resource for each other. It is important to build assessment in from the start as you plan and deliver primary languages provision. This approach to assessment keys into existing effective practice and works very much to the benefit of the children as regards their individual learning needs and as a whole learning group, and when it is firmly linked to framework objectives, then teachers, and indeed the pupils, know exactly what is being assessed.

# 6 The role of the primary languages subject leader

This chapter discusses how to:

- work towards a whole-school collaborative programme of language teaching and learning
- establish, develop and sustain a successful programme of primary language learning
- define and develop the role and responsibilities of the primary languages subject leader
- contribute meaningfully to primary languages subject leadership in the first years of teaching
- create a realistic and effective modern languages policy for the primary school
- begin to develop management and leadership capability, and to support professional learning in the context of primary language subject leadership.

## Introduction

Currently, subject leadership of primary languages remains fairly undeveloped, with those who adopt the role having only very limited understanding either of the target language, language teaching methodologies, or even subject leadership itself. In terms of modern languages, many primary schools have little or even no existing capacity and thus, even rudimentary French or German, for example, becomes the driving factor in the choice of both the subject leader, and the choice of language to be taught. We are in a situation where newly-qualified primary teachers may find themselves *de facto* subject leaders in their first years of teaching because they may be the only subject specialists, or the best trained in language teaching methodology, and thus deemed to be the most competent for the role. This is not an inappropriate situation *per se* – while newly-qualified teachers are entitled to a robust programme of support, assuming or sharing responsibility for subject leadership can be an integral part of their continuing professional development, and allow them to apply their newly-acquired knowledge and skills in a very practical way. This sits well with contemporary models of leadership in schools – it is often shared and distributed, with a focus on learning for both pupils *and* teachers. 'Leadership' is no longer defined as the preserve of a single individual, nor solely of a senior leadership/management team – it is dispersed, distributed, shared within and across the whole school. This increases what Sergiovanni calls 'leadership density' (2001: 112), hence the number of people sharing in leadership responsibilities and decision-making and also in contributing ideas. It is a collective endeavour that makes optimal use of the social and intellectual capital of all individuals, giving decision-making powers, authority and opportunities to those who can make the most effective contribution at any one time. In such an endeavour, there is the possibility for all teachers, newly-trained or more experienced, to share leadership at various times and for real collaborative working. Whitaker (1993) identifies the need for schools to move from 'individual responsibility' to 'shared responsibility':

> Effective teamwork is the hallmark of most successful organisations. When teams can be brought together to serve the needs of the moment quicker and more effective results can be achieved. Tying down individuals into separate and discrete areas of responsibility can inhibit the capacity of the organisation to respond successfully to ... change. It can also suppress the qualities of imagination and creativity that tend to be aroused when people come together in task teams.
>
> (1993: 88)

Thus, in the construct of 'shared responsibility', primary languages subject leaders need to see themselves not just as middle leaders within the whole-school structure but as subject team leaders, working with all those contributing to languages provision collaboratively, be they other class teachers, Teaching Assistants, Foreign Language Assistants and, of course, the Head who is a key member of the team. Harris writes that a prime purpose of the team is in: 'constructing meaning and knowledge collectively and collaboratively' (Harris et al. 2003: 75) which we interpret to mean that the team, guided by the subject leader, gives conceptual shape to primary languages, establishing a strong identity and an effective pedagogy which must be a priority of languages subject leadership.

## A shared responsibility: ensuring sustainability of the school's languages programme

The last large-scale attempt (see Introduction) to include languages in the primary curriculum highlighted a number of areas that contributed to the demise of the scheme. Central to these were the 'organization and teaching problems' it posed. Sustaining even robust language programmes became an increasing barrier to its longer-term success, and this is being replicated today. As McLachlan (2009b) points out:

> To sustain the [National Languages] strategy as a long-term educational goal, it is clear that having the teachers to teach it is central to its success. Currently, teacher supply appears to be inadequate, with responsibility for language teaching across schools often resting on the shoulders of a single teacher. Where this is the case, then sustainability within that school is in severe jeopardy, a warning issued by Low in 1999 and again by Martin in 2000.

In July 2005, Ofsted published an interim evaluation of progress in 10 local authorities (LA) in the 'Pathfinder Project' (*Implementing Languages Entitlement in Primary Schools: An Evaluation of Progress in Ten Pathfinder LEAs,* Ofsted, July 2005) and found that the most successful initiatives were underpinned by 'strong, clear leadership and management' (2005: 3). Based on its evaluation, the report recommends that primary schools should 'ensure that the school improvement plan includes planning for PMFL [Primary Modern Foreign Languages]' (2005: 5) which should include among other things 'clearly identified strategies for sustaining PMFL' and 'procedures for monitoring the quality of PMFL teaching and learning' (2005: 5). The report concluded that in many schools, 'uncertainty' is impeding development of languages programmes. As one Deputy Head explained: 'I think the ideal model would be each individual teacher providing it, but being realistic, people move on, so you can't depend on it being taught in every individual year group anyway' (McLachlan 2009b). Where a primary school relies heavily on the support of the local secondary schools or SLC for its languages programme, it essentially has to deal with an additional layer of complexity in terms of suitable staff supply. McLachlan (2009b) highlights the problems one such primary school faced:

> [The Head] told me of the problems his school were facing continuing their programme firstly because the peripatetic languages teacher provided by the local Specialist Language College had left, and secondly, because the SLC itself was awaiting confirmation of its continued status: '... it could create hellish headaches if, like, a month into September they're not able to appoint anyone to replace her [the peripatetic teacher] ... and they've only just had the acknowledgement through to say that they will get the next stage of their funding for language ... so they've only found that out literally in the last couple of days, so we have to wait for them first of all to see if they've got the funding ..., and then see who they can appoint.

The building and nurturing of a skilled and committed team are important in ensuring that all colleagues feel supported in sharing skills and competences and, crucially, for the sustainability of languages. One Head, for example, said: 'Presently I do not have concerns as I have a suitably qualified and competent staff. If my "key player" were to leave, I do not know how French would then be arranged.' Another Head arguing in favour of languages teaching by class generalist teachers to 'spread' subject ownership suggested that: 'If class teachers were enabled, French would become part of the daily routine and be used across the curriculum.'

## Prioritizing teaching and learning languages: ensuring subject status

Succession must always be in place and there must be a team of at least two to consolidate and develop the place of primary languages. In many instances (Driscoll,

Jones and Macrory 2004), it has been found that languages have been – and sometimes still are – a fragile entity in the primary curriculum, marginalized, a Cinderella subject and thus in need of robust subject leadership to secure an equitable position to which our young learners are entitled. Several subject leaders interviewed about the topic reported on the perceived 'dispensability' of French: 'Timetable changes often lead to the cancellation of French'; 'Unfortunately, it is often the first subject to get dropped in a busy week' and, in contradiction with the point about class teachers above: 'Class teachers who deliver their own French lessons sometimes replace French with another subject.' Equality of subject esteem in the primary curriculum will not happen without equally robust support from the senior leadership and, as a *sine qua non*, the Head who ultimately has the position power to make things happen. This view was forcefully expressed by one Head thus: 'It is very easy to let things slip and I do acknowledge my strategic role in ensuring staff are available and in checking that it happens. The Head needs to give it status and check planning to help embed French across the curriculum.' Another Head similarly talked of the need to be a 'champion' for a subject: 'You need the headteacher to commit to manage French or there is the danger it will be put aside. Like all subjects, it needs a champion and preferably some personal experience.' Similar views were expressed by all the Heads we asked. In raising the issue of 'status' and being a 'champion', there is a clear understanding of the position, resource and personal power of headteachers to 'make things happen'. In the next section, we look at the functions and responsibilities in the role of the subject leader who also has the potential to 'make things happen', in the classroom, especially when fully supported by the Head of the school.

## Defining the role of the subject leader

The Teacher Training Agency (now the Training and Development Agency for Schools) in 1998 published National Standards for subject leadership in which the core purpose of that leadership is defined as:

> to provide professional leadership and management for a subject to secure high quality teaching, effective use of resources and improved standards of learning and achievement for all pupils within the context of the school's overall aims and policies, and commitment to high achievement and effective teaching and learning.
>
> (1998: 5)

It identified four key areas of subject leadership:

1  *Strategic direction and development of the subject* – within the context of the school's aims and policies, subject leaders develop and implement subject policies, plans, targets and practices.
2  *Teaching and learning* – subject leaders secure and sustain effective teaching of the subject, evaluate the quality of teaching and standards of pupils' achievements and set targets for improvement.

3   *Leading and managing staff* – subject leaders provide to all those with involvement or support of the subject, the support, challenge, information and development necessary to sustain motivation and secure improvement in teaching.

4   *Efficient and effective deployment of staff and resources* – subject leaders identify appropriate resources for the subject and ensure that they are used efficiently, effectively and safely.

While current models of languages subject leadership appear to be diverse, a robust framework is emerging, with clear reference to the national standards, and more importantly, with key concordances between schools. One subject leader defines her responsibilities as follows:

- Auditing, organizing and controlling the budget for French resources.
- Ensuring supplies of the pupils' books are ordered.
- Supporting the Headteacher in organizing the residential visit.
- To write the risk assessment for the visit.
- Organizing the pupils' school trip diaries.
- To be responsible for the school display of French materials.
- Forging and encouraging new links between the school and our link primary school in France.
- Liaison with secondary schools.
- Researching and making available other resources including ICT.
- Organizing assessment and recording assessment data.

Another subject leader describes his role as working with colleagues to undertake the following:

- Understand the requirements of the National Curriculum.
- Prepare policy documents, curriculum plans and schemes of work.
- Encourage staff to develop language competence.
- Model language lessons for colleagues.
- Collect teaching resources.
- Develop assessment and recording policy.

## Developing leadership capability and supporting professional learning

Subject Leadership involves being committed to ongoing personal professional development, particularly in terms of developing leadership capability, as well as assuming responsibility for the professional development of other members of school staff. How we define 'subject leadership' and its integral remit of 'subject management' in primary languages will be central to its longer-term success. Whitaker (1993: 74) defines the scope of leadership and management as follows:

| Leadership | Management |
|---|---|
| is concerned with | |
| • personal and interpersonal behaviour | • orderly structures |
| • focus on the future | • maintaining day-to-day functions |
| • change and development | • ensuring that work gets done |
| • quality | • monitoring outcomes and results |
| • effectiveness | • efficiency |

Whitaker (1993: 76) (citing Adair) characterizes five key features in effective leadership:

1  *Direction* – leaders are concerned to find ways forward, to generate a clear sense of movement and direction. This may involve identifying new goals, new services and new structures.
2  *Inspiration* – leaders have ideas and articulate thoughts that are strong motivators for the working team, creating a directional energy.
3  *Building teams* – leaders see teams as the natural and most effective form of management and spend their time in encouraging and coaching.
4  *Example* – leadership is example and it is not only what leaders do that affects the others in the organization, but how they do it.
5  *Acceptance* – managers can be designated by title, but do not become leaders until that appointment is ratified in the hearts and minds of the followers.

Thus, the effective primary languages Subject Leader will have qualities, skills and vision for the subject that go beyond the level of subject knowledge, and be able to transmit those qualities, skills and vision convincingly to the whole-school team.

When creating a programme of development for INSET or other professional learning opportunities, subject leaders must have not only clearly defined goals for the subject itself, but also an understanding of the current skills and interests of colleagues. Conducting a training needs audit will inform the outline of an initial framework within which the Subject Leader can address the current interests and skills of staff, and enable them to develop new skills in a non-threatening environment. Whitaker (1993: 57) emphasizes the importance of identifying the key purposes of a programme of professional learning and suggests the following as a template in its initial design:

**inform** the need to **know**
**familiarise** the need to **understand**
**adapt** the need to **change**
**develop** the need to **extend**
**implement** the need to **innovate**
**encourage** the need to **build confidence**
**train** the need to **acquire new skills**
**reflect** the need to **make sense of experience**
**explore** the need to **consider possibilities**
**review** the need to **assess and evaluate**

## Activity

1   Prior to your next school-based training, draw up a training/skills audit for school staff. Think about what you would most need to know in order to create a relevant programme of training. Ask members of staff to volunteer to complete the audit, ensuring that they understand why you are conducting this activity.

2   Read and reflect carefully upon the audits you have been able to conduct in school. Draw up an outline for an initial 3-hour INSET programme to present to your training group. After your presentation, you will identify the core purpose(s) of the programme, and explain the rationale for its content (the results of the audit), with specific reference to Whitaker's and Adair's definition of leadership.

3   Building on the outline in (2), develop the programme further to cover a number of sessions throughout the school year. Think carefully about how much time a school and its staff can reasonably devote to training, and how you might prioritize content.

## Managing resources: 'tidying the cupboard' and more

The National Standards have a strong focus on ensuring and monitoring the quality of learning and teaching. It requires a learning-centred leadership defined by Earley and Weindling as: 'about learning – pupil, adult (teachers, staff and governors), orga- nizational learning and leadership networks and teaching' (2004: 14). The standards reflect a huge shift from what Burrows (2004, for the NCSL) identified as the 'tidy- ing the cupboard' definition of subject leadership role in which teachers busy them- selves and become preoccupied with their teaching resources, towards a role that is clearly focused on leading learning and teaching. We would not, however, denigrate the 'primary languages cupboard' outright for we have seen some splendid cupboards, es- pecially in smaller schools, full of resources, with teaching lesson files, policies, sample of children's work and assessment files accessible to all in the subject team. Building a well-stocked languages resource cupboard, tailored to the particular needs of both teachers and pupils, and evaluating their effectiveness and relevance on a yearly basis, thus remains an important part of the role.

## Teachers talking

### Being a primary languages subject leader and developing a programme of language learning

Q: *Can you define the role of the primary languages subject leader?*

A: *Subject Leader A:* First and foremost it's to monitor and lead your subject across the school, giving help and ideas as well as ensuring policy and paperwork is up to date. I think subject leaders should lead by example showing good practice in their own classrooms including setting up displays, as well as showing interest in what is happening in other classrooms. They should be on the lookout for relevant training courses, then feed back to staff. I think it's important that languages subject leaders keep themselves and the rest of the staff informed of current issues, and to audit resources keeping staff informed of what there is, and how they might use it. Also they have to monitor staff, helping them with their professional development and provide training where necessary including INSET.

In terms of administrative responsibilities, certainly subject leaders have to update the policy and schemes of work on an annual basis to ensure they're all still relevant to the school and the pupils. Monitoring teaching and learning is crucial if subject leaders are to retain an overview of issues and progress both for pupils and staff, and to track pupils where appropriate, identifying gifted and talented pupils and provide extension where possible (i.e. we have been able to offer Latin to a G&T group in Yr 5 this year).

A: *Subject Leader B:* A subject leader promotes and nurtures a subject within a school and provides teachers with the resources, knowledge, skills and understanding to deliver lessons in their area to a high standard. You have to develop an effective curriculum, manage the timetabling of sessions and the professional development not only of staff, but of yourself! Additionally, raising the profile of the subject within groups of stakeholders is very important.

Q: *What are your targets for the development of your languages programme?*

A: *Subject Leader A:* We'll be increasing teaching time to 45 minutes a week, and encouraging more staff to at least 'give it a go'. I'm also keen to encourage staff to do more between lessons, i.e. not just have 'discrete' language lessons, but to use the language as often as possible during the day. In terms of G&T, I'd like to be able to include other language learning opportunities. I'm also keen to develop training with both staff and trainees in our Partnership, and to buy more resources – in particular Big Books for shared reading. This year I'll be exploring how we might develop a more formal method of assessing pupil progress, and this will also inform the quality of information we are able to pass on to our secondary schools. I'm also looking at how colleagues at other schools have embedded written work into their programmes.

A: *Subject Leader B:* My main priority is to make staff self-sufficient in teaching Spanish from Reception to Year 6, providing pupils with a solid base of knowledge to take to secondary schools, and instilling a positive attitude to languages in pupils.

Q: *What are your plans for achieving these targets?*

A: *Subject Leader A:* Developing links with our High Schools to include some of their teachers coming in to develop other languages, and hopefully to provide some more funding for resources. We're working on in-house training by making it a priority on the SIP, and are maintaining strong links with our local HEI provider. I want to develop a form of assessment that doesn't make the lessons less interesting, yet gives clearer overview of pupil progress.

A: *Subject Leader B:* I'll be informing staff about professional development opportunities and encourage them to exploit those opportunities. I'll ensure that the FLA has a defined role in supporting staff in their professional development and plays an active role in promoting languages in the school. I want to make lessons fun through curriculum and delivery, while providing pupils with a structured programme of teaching that will provide them with practical knowledge they can build on at secondary school – excellence and enjoyment!

## Activity

Based on one of your observation or professional placement schools, how would you characterize the role of the Subject Leader? Suggest ways the current languages and professional development programme could be improved, giving reasons.

## What do beginning primary languages subject leaders need to know?

As noted above, primary languages offer the newly-qualified teacher an almost unprecedented opportunity to lead, or at least contribute significantly, to subject leadership even in the first year of teaching. As you prepare for your first appointment interviews, and subsequently your first year of teaching, use the following as a reference framework:

In the context of the core competences outlined by the TTA (1998) above, the effective primary subject leader will have:

- an understanding of the national vision for languages (The National Languages Strategy);

- knowledge of the KS2 Framework for Languages and how this may support learning across the primary curriculum;
- knowledge of the non-statutory QCA Schemes of Work for French, German and Spanish;
- an awareness of potential assessment strategies, including the National Curriculum level descriptors (at least Levels 1–4) and the Languages Ladder;
- an understanding of language teaching strategies appropriate to the KS2 context;
- an awareness of languages across the KS2–KS3 bridge;
- an understanding of the professional development needs of colleagues, and an ability to create a programme of training to address those needs.

They will assume responsibility for:

- the creation of an appropriate languages policy in line with the School Improvement Plan and the whole-school vision for learning;
- planning for progression and continuity in language learning;
- monitoring outcomes of the languages programme;
- evaluating the effectiveness of the current policy, and developing new languages policy;
- ensuring a supply of suitably trained staff;
- sustaining the languages programme;
- the acquisition of appropriate teaching and learning resources;
- the acquisition of appropriate staff development resources;
- the effective management of transfer and transition from KS2 to KS3.

They will be committed to:

- networking with colleagues in other local schools, and across the LA;
- exploring the potential of international links;
- the development of sound teaching and learning in the subject;
- personal professional development, and supporting the professional learning of colleagues.

## Leading beyond the school

Subject leaders will naturally spend most of their time in the day-to-day business of the school. However, schools these days more often than not work in area groups, clusters and networks, not just for the sake of collegiality or to share 'good practice', valuable though these are, but also, as Hopkins and Jackson assert (2003: 94), to help schools share and understand 'good process' – the capacity-creating process that leads to 'best practice'. Subject leaders can reap the benefit of the support of peers and can learn much from each other, thereby developing subject knowledge and subject leadership capability. It is clear that the National Standards for subject leadership relate to issues of standards generally and school improvement, a big brief for lone subject leaders who can benefit from the support structure of the peer group by making connections and synergizing priorities. Such networks in fact go beyond the local school cluster for primary languages subject leadership has its own national infrastructure for professional development, e.g. provided by CILT and ALL, and innumerable opportunities for international connections like no other subject. Such connections are often the jewel in the crown of languages provision and highly motivating for both teachers and pupils and, as such, are explored in Chapter 10.

## Developing a languages policy for the primary school

A key activity in the subject leader's role is the development of the school modern languages policy, which should encompass both the vision for the subject itself, as well as the whole-school vision.

---

### Activity

**Part 1**

Read the language policy exemplar in Box 6.1, noting what you consider to be its key strengths, and why. Reflect particularly on how clear you consider its vision and guidance to be, and to what extent it provides a clear framework for the effective development of both teacher and pupil learning

**Part 2**

Based on one of your professional placement schools, write a languages policy to present to your group, explaining its context and rationale. Your policy should make specific reference to teaching and learning, assessment and transfer/transition arrangements

---

# Box 6.1 Elmridge Primary School modern foreign languages policy

*Learning through success*

## Introduction

Learning a foreign language shows a willingness to be responsive to the culture whose language is being studied. Besides promoting the acquisition of linguistic skills, language also fosters tolerance and respect for others, and an appreciation of their skills and achievements.

*Elmridge Primary School* acknowledges the importance of cross-cultural understanding and this is reflected in the inclusion of modern languages as an integral part of the school curriculum.

## 1. The aims of modern foreign language teaching

- to foster tolerance and respect for other cultures
- to develop the ability to communicate with native speakers of other languages
- to develop awareness of our geographical location and culture within a wider European and world context
- to give pupils an insight into the workings of their own language through comparative language study
- to promote respect and integration within the class through role play, pair work and team games
- to support the transition to Key Stage 3 where language learning is compulsory
- to improve skills in other subjects through cross-curricular links

## 2. The place of modern foreign languages in the school curriculum

Modern foreign languages – Spanish at present – is taught to Key Stage 1 and 2 pupils in Years 2, 3, 4, 5 and 6 on a weekly basis. Lessons are currently taught by the Modern Foreign Languages Coordinator, the Year 2 and the Year 3 teacher. The duration of the lessons are 30 minutes in Years 2, 3 and 4 progressing to 40 minutes in Years 5 and 6. The Modern Foreign Language Coordinator arranges to swap with the Year 4 and 5 teachers at the timetabled slot to enable each class to receive its modern language lesson.

Spanish has recently been the focus of a school theme week where each class performed a song, rhyme or role play on a Spanish theme in a Friday assembly, demonstrating the areas and skills they had been working on during the week.

## 3. The scheme of work

The school has its own scheme of work which is designed to follow the skill development set out in the National Languages Framework. A variety of media are used in the teaching including authentic songs and rhymes, video, interactive whiteboards. Lessons are designed to be pacy and fun. In the first two years of teaching, the Sale Grammar School scheme of work is used, which is designed to fulfil the criteria laid down by the Framework for Languages. Each unit provides lesson objectives and outcomes as well as suggested activities. It also contains a list of recommended resources, suggested links with other subjects and criteria for assessment.

In Year 3 of teaching, the pupils are following the QCA scheme of work topics which enables more cross-curricular links to be formed.

## 4. Planning

Medium-term planning lists the objectives that the teacher aims to cover in a particular term as well as the resources that will be required to achieve each objective or cluster of objectives. The weekly planning provides the lessons' objectives along with a lot of activities and learning outcomes. Differentiation is recorded and any resources are listed. Cross-curricular links, if present, are also highlighted. Lesson plans are available for Years 1 and 2 of teaching. These plans will need to be adapted for the requirements of each class.

## 5. Teaching

Teaching methods aim to develop the pupils' ability in all four skills: listening, speaking, reading and writing. The weighting of these skills changes between Years 2 and 6 with the first two years of lessons being more speaking and listening based.

Pupils' skills are developed within the context of the Sale Grammar Scheme and the QCA topics with links made to the Modern Languages Framework and its five strands. Initially, the topics are not as evident, as the lessons will be aimed at giving the pupils interesting and authentic experiences of the sound of the language using songs and rhymes. In addition, pupils will develop a basic knowledge of classroom vocabulary and phrases. The aim for the first year will be to enable the pupils to develop their pronunciation and their ear for the language and to gain confidence responding to classroom instructions in the target language. The goal in the first two years is to nurture a love for and interest in language learning without vocabulary acquisition constituting the main focus. Many traditional Spanish songs and rhymes are brought into the lessons to give the pupils' learning experiences an authentic Spanish feel and enrich the cultural experiences.

With Spanish now being taught across five year groups, many topic areas will be revisited. The aim of the teaching is that the pupils do not simply learn skills and vocabulary relating solely to individual topics, but learn transferable skills that can be built upon throughout the age ranges. In Years 4, 5 and 6 more topic-based work is incorporated into lessons but the main focus of lessons is nevertheless skill development as opposed to simply vocabulary acquisition.

Texts are introduced (for example, Big Books) where pupils encounter new vocabulary in isolation. Reading material relating directly to topics being studied also acts to galvanize pupils' understanding of words and phrases. Links can be easily made between the modern foreign language scheme of work and the National Literacy Strategy, and exploited in reading sessions.

Writing takes on a more significant role in the junior years and pupils have established an e-mail link with a Spanish school which offers new opportunities for linking writing and ICT.

Teaching techniques include:

- the presentation of vocabulary using OHP and flashcards
- repetition of words and phrases
- songs
- videos
- ICT – CD-ROMs and PowerPoint and website activities
- role play
- reading of Big Books
- playing cassettes/CDs
- games

Pupils work individually, in pairs and in groups. Most of the teaching takes place in a mixed ability environment. The structure of the teaching sessions does not follow a fixed format; it varies. Nevertheless, objectives are shared with the pupils in each lesson and a short plenary takes place at the end of each lesson to assess and review the pupils' learning.

## 6. Equal opportunities

All pupils, regardless of ability, race or gender are given equal access to resources. Classroom Management takes into account such issues, and uses curriculum materials which are not biased.

## 7. ICT resources

Some software is now available for the pupils to use in the ICT suite. CD-ROMs, website and e-mail are all relevant to the QCA scheme of work. Furthermore information can be presented, edited and re-organized by word processing and PowerPoint. Pupils are regularly e-mailing Spain through the Epals network.

## 8. Monitoring

Continuity and progression are ensured by the scrutiny of work recorded and the evaluation of lessons, techniques and methodology. Progress through attainment targets can be checked using testing and other assessment results from Years 2 to 6.

## 9. Assessment

Learning objectives or clusters of learning objectives may necessitate more than one lesson to achieve. When the learning outcomes have been completed, pupils will be assessed against the main objective of the lesson or series of lessons. Each of the 12 QCA units also has end of unit expectation which provides broad descriptions of achievement. This enables the teacher to look at a child's progress over a number of lessons against expected attainment.

At the end of Key Stage 2, pupils are given a level according to the attainment target level descriptions described in the National Curriculum.

## 10. Management and the subject leader's role

The subject leader's role involves working with colleagues to undertake the following:

- understand the requirements of the National Curriculum
- prepare policy documents, curriculum plans and schemes of work
- encourage staff to develop language competence
- model language lessons for colleagues
- collect teaching resources
- develop assessment and recording policy

## 11. Resources

Classroom and other resources are organized to promote effective learning in modern foreign languages. Resources are stored centrally on shelves in the computer suite.

All the resources currently in use have been employed by the staff after checking that they in no way promote racial or sexual stereotyping. They also match the age and ability of the children they are used with.

## 12. Review

This policy will be reviewed on an annual basis after liaison with the Senior Management Team.

# Conclusion

We would characterize the primary languages subject leader as a middle leader located within a paradigm of *distributed leadership*. The profile and status of both the subject, and the subject leader, must evolve to provide a firm foundation for language learning in the primary curriculum. The success of a subject in a school depends to a great extent upon the quality of leadership of that subject. The role involves both strategic direction and development of the subject and the management and leadership of a team, i.e. all those involved in some way with primary languages provision. As one Head said: 'I do not want any one teacher to be isolated in her (*sic*) role but to be team leader and leader of learning of a task team.' Monitoring outcomes, and supporting teachers in the delivery of quality provision in teaching and effective learning outcomes are key elements of the subject leader's role. Most of all, the role needs to be understood as an ongoing dialogue and collaborative team effort concerned with the quality of teaching and learning.

# 7 Planning for continuity and progression

## Transition from KS2 to KS3

---

This chapter discusses how to:

- plan for progression in language learning from KS2 to KS3
- listen to and discuss pupils' needs and expectations
- collaborate successfully with secondary languages teachers to ensure continuity and appropriate learning challenges
- build 'bridges' between primary and secondary on the basis of joint transitional planning.

---

## Introduction

Despite the disappointing conclusion of the Burstall project (see Chapter 1), many primary schools continued to offer some form of language learning, though it has sometimes been a vulnerable subject in the curriculum and considered rather 'lightweight' (Driscoll et al. 2004). Often, languages have been seen as 'fun' and something of a light relief to counterbalance the impositions of the National Curriculum, most notably national testing, as one Headteacher commented: 'It's going to be about them learning songs, learning rhymes … it's a relief from the grind.'

While it is important that both teachers and young learners enjoy the language learning process, it is equally important that languages have at least the same status as other foundation subjects. Current policy dictates that from 2010 schools will be obliged to provide an hour a week of language learning, though discrete language lessons are themselves not mandatory. However, there is some indication that this will change at the next Primary Review, with Dearing's recent recommendation that 'languages become part of the statutory curriculum at KS2 in primary schools, when it is next reviewed' (*Languages Review*, Dearing and King 2007: 10). Thus, the belief in the lifelong educational value of languages on the part of the primary languages community of practice, coupled with a long-term and clearly defined commitment from educational policy-makers, it is likely that in the very near future, languages will gain status as a subject in the mainstream primary curriculum, and hopefully, in the national consciousness.

While children benefit from continuity in all subjects at this crucial transition stage, continuity is essential for children's motivation and progression in their language learning. At the end of KS3, students are able to discontinue language study and the temptation to do so is considerable if the subject is perceived as repetitive, non-progressive and difficult. The issue of severe grading remains a very trenchant issue for the languages teaching community. Secondary language teachers may feel disadvantaged (Jones and Coffey 2006; Jones 2010) because of their perception that their primary colleagues have all the 'fun bits' and teach pupils at a stage when they are very receptive to new language. This is partly based on a misconception and a lack of understanding of the primary context.

---

## Teachers talking

A teacher discusses the transition phase.

A lot of secondary teachers seem to perceive this as just playing, they don't see a lot of the grammar we put in and also what levels the children come out at, some children are really extremely gifted, some are very talented, and they perhaps regress for the first year or so until they sort of catch up again and it's difficult because you think ... we're really flogging them, and really getting them to a good standard, and you want them to carry on with that sort of progression, and you just hope that it continues but you know that in Languages it's not happening ... you're sort of almost wiping the slate clean and they're regressing and you may have problems with children you know not wanting to carry on with it because they're getting bored with it, so that's maybe a real fear of doing from Yr 2 to Yr 6 is if they go to different schools, and of course they go to so many different secondary schools, even if one school's doing a really great job of doing it, the others might not be but it's still ... but we can't not do it because of that, you know we feel passionate about it so we feel that the secondary schools have to work with us, rather than stopping the primary schools.

---

In a study that tracked pupils from Year 6 to the end of Year 7, Bolster et al. (2004: 39) reported a 'complex and somewhat contradictory picture', mirroring Burstall's findings some 35 years ago and Jones' findings more recently (2010). The researchers concluded that 'opportunities which exist for building on primary language learning are largely wasted' which appears to have 'contributed to the somewhat disillusioned attitude of a certain number of secondary school pupils' (Bolster et al. 2004: 38).

It may well be that there is an equal lack of understanding of the secondary context on the part of primary practitioners, which demonstrates the urgent need for primary and secondary teachers to engage in ongoing dialogue about learning and teaching and to work together to develop a shared understanding of learners' needs and capabilities and to plan accordingly. On the basis of this collaboration, pupils' learning progression can be increasingly assured. We would also argue that where a more structured approach to assessment is embedded into primary languages practice, this will facilitate the communication of individual pupil progress. We have found that, as yet, schools are communicating little or no information about individual pupil attainment in languages, and where formal statements of achievement are passed to the secondary school, it was felt that the secondary schools still did not address those prior attainments in their own teaching. Indeed, with no formal or standardized assessment procedures in place, this will continue to be an issue: how can relevant information on attainment be gathered and communicated to the secondary school, and to what extent can we expect the secondary school to act on that information?

Burstall too found that 'at the secondary level, almost all organizational problems can be traced to the fact that most schools received a mixed intake of pupils with varying degrees of previous contact . . . but who are nevertheless expected to strive towards the same goals at a reasonably uniform pace' (Burstall et al. 1974: 245). Equally importantly, measuring either attainment in language learning in particular, or impact on learning in general, in these circumstances becomes something of a pipe-dream – where there is no systematic national programme of learning, and no systematic national assessment procedures in place, we cannot hope to evaluate learning meaningfully.

## A period of many transitions

There is a tendency to think in terms of transition as the 'primary to secondary' transition. This is certainly a major point of transition but there are, in fact, many transitions in a child's schooling at the primary stage such as:

- Home to school
- Pre-school to Reception
- Reception to KS1
- KS1 to KS2
- Learning through play to structured curriculum
- Child talk to school talk
- Teacher monitoring to national testing.

There are many other subtler transitions that create a dynamic of change as pupils mature and are able to engage with learning experiences appropriate to their age range and developing cognition. In the first instance, however, transition is a period of considerable anxiety, and one that features many 'discontinuities' in pupil learning (Galton et al. 1999), as some teachers fail to build on what pupils already know and cling to the belief that a fresh start is the most appropriate starting point in learning. The welcome, settling in and induction for Yr 6 and Yr 7 are often extremely well planned by schools and fulfil some of the 'bridges' or approaches identified by Galton et al. (1999) whose crossings need to be well planned to ensure a smooth transition:

1  *Bureaucratic*: the formal liaison between schools, usually at Senior Leadership level.
2  *Social and personal*: the creation of social links prior to and after transfer, and at induction.
3  *Curriculum*: the sharing of content to be taught.
4  *Pedagogic*: the development of an understanding of how pupils are taught.
5  *Managing learning*: a consideration of how each pupil can be helped to manage the transition in the light of achievement and needs and how to move forward.

In language learning, the curriculum, pedagogic and managing learning bridges are currently underdeveloped – in other words, the learning bridge that recognizes 'pupils' needs and capacity to develop a language about thinking about learning and about themselves as learners' (Galton et al. 1999: 3). Where primary pupils have experienced effective and embedded formative assessment based on an AfL approach in the primary school (and, as stated in the chapter on assessment, many primary pupils have done so), the pupils take, as one Head called it, 'suitcases of learning skills' to secondary school that can be exploited by Yr 7 teachers in order to progress learning. Even when such continuity is missing, there is evidence (Jones 2010) that pupils have the capability for transferring their learning skills to the new secondary context and can 'figure things out' for themselves. This is exactly what we want the young languages learner to be able to do, to operate as effective strategic language learners and as agents in their own progress. When talking to Yr 6 pupils, we have found them to be articulate, confident and excited about continuing their language learning as we see in the next section.

When dealing with transitional and transfer issues, it is important to listen to pupils' views, ideas and concerns. Transition is not just an abstraction or something that just happens at the end of Year 6; it is a very real break in pupils' lives and a prospect that inspires feelings of anxiety as well as excitement. Indeed, Year 6 pupils, when interviewed, invariably reveal mixed feelings about the imminent move to secondary schools.

## Pupils talking: Year 6 pupils' needs and expectations

These comments, from pupils in a class of Year 6 children in a mixed primary school in their final term, about whether they were looking forward to going to secondary school are quite typical of these feelings:

Yes, and no, yes, it will be a challenge, no, I am not comfortable about the idea.
Yes, because we will get to make more friends and be able to play full contact rugby.
No, because my sister says you can get consequences [*sic*] for doing nothing.

*Asked about whether they were looking forward to language learning at secondary school, the children's answers were mixed:*

Yes, because I have learnt a language at primary school so I think it won't be very hard.
Yes, I am looking forward because I enjoy learning a new language.

*and*

No, because I think you have to learn how to write in a foreign language.
No, the homework would do my head in.

*In response to a question about whether they thought their primary language learning would help them with languages at secondary school, there was considerable consensus and the children gave their reasons:*

Yes, because if we learn a language at primary school it makes us aware of what we have to do at secondary school.
Yes, I think it will help because we have learnt how to remember to pronounce words.
Maybe, yes, because we have learnt the basics and got the flow, no, because we will be learning more difficult words and have to write down the words rather than say the words aloud.

*Providing a good argument for introducing writing at primary school (see Chapter 4), we further probed about the nature of the progress they were expecting to make. The children answered:*

Yes, I think we will make progress because we will have more than one lesson a week.
Yes, because I am making very good progress at primary school and from what I have heard the teaching at secondary school is very good.
Yes, because then I will be able to have a conversation with foreign people.
I think we will because we will learn more and harder things which will challenge us more.

Discussing their concerns, they were anxious about reports they had heard about 'strict and harsh' teachers as well as issues in languages concerning 'harder work', 'more writing' and 'new languages'. When asked, Year 6 pupils had sensible ideas about what teachers could do to help them with the learning transition when they begin in Year 7:

- Give me some time to take it all in.
- Revise some things we have done to make sure we are steady on it.
- Maybe occasionally repeat things in the new subject but not the whole old subject again.
- Set up a programme that will help you how to write and memorize things clearly.

- Could you talk about my progress?
- I would like a bit of help when I get stuck.
- Could the children do more than learning just things and names of objects!
- I'd like to talk about interesting topics like how children and teenagers feel about growing up, and if they have the same ideas and problems as us.
- I hope we don't have to keep colouring flags in and drawing pictures of animals and things. We've been doing that over and over again and it's so boring, I'm beginning to hate French.
- I like singing songs and things, but not all the time. I'd like to be able to say and understand more things.

This is valuable information for teachers when discussing transitional planning across the Key Stages.

---

### Activity

In small groups, take each of the Year 6 pupil statements and consider the implications for teaching and learning. What is the nature of the pupils' concerns? What are their needs? How can these be met?

---

Throughout this book, we are working on the basis of language teachers as inherently reflective about their work and with an ongoing sense of inquiry. Indeed, we suggest that teachers are natural researchers in their own classrooms and have a rich variety of data available to them with their learners, their learning behaviours and the learning outcomes (see the Epilogue). It is both interesting and insightful for primary teachers to talk to pupils in Year 7, either their own children when they have moved up to secondary school or others in linked schools, to listen to the children's reflections and compare them to their expectations, concerns and hopes that they expressed as primary pupils.

## The Year 7 perspective

In our sample of Year 7s, the pupils told us that they were enjoying their secondary school experiences of language learning in the 1st term and that they were covering many topics they had done in the primary school. An analysis of Yr 7 textbooks and the topics covered in Years 5 and 6 indeed revealed a large amount of common ground. As to whether the pupils felt they had progressed from Yr 6 to Yr 7, they were unanimous that they had:

> French is easier, we speak better, we understand more French, we read better and we know more words.

We do better conversations, we can spell, the more you learn the better you get. We know more generally than in primary school. The teacher helps us and we revise. We do the same but different.

It's good. We first went over what we knew but harder. We prefer working as a class but we do lots of pair work. Occasionally it is going over the same stuff.

We have done so much, we do a lot in a lesson. It was hard at the start as we didn't understand the teacher but she kept pecking away.

Where transition in terms of the learning and pedagogic 'bridges' is well planned, it is much to the pupils' advantage and provides the essential agenda for a conversation about learning at transition. Too often the conversation has been restricted to procedural issues and yet, as the following language teachers talking show, there are crucial issues to discuss in order to deal with misconception and to find a way to ensure consolidation as well as increasingly cognitively challenging work that the pupils need in order to progress. Revision should be tapered to identified needs, and a programme of learning in itself, and not comprise teaching *ab initio* material and calling it 'revision'. In the following section, teachers identify and discuss some of those issues.

## Teachers talking

### A primary school languages teacher

Q: *How would you describe the role of the primary–secondary liaison teacher?*

A: The primary–secondary liaison teacher should be in regular contact with the high school throughout the year and not just in the summer term. There should be discussions on the way languages are taught, how high schools can support the primaries and even the sharing of resources. Information needs to be passed on at the transition stage but this needs to be practical useful information and not just the 'portfolio/passport' that has been completed by pupils as this isn't always a true reflection of what is known by a particular pupil.

Q: *What primary languages information do you currently pass on and what ideally would you think it helpful to pass on to the secondary school?*

A: Not a lot really in terms of languages because we're not following a set curriculum so we can't say, well, we've done that and that, but not done that yet. I'd like to be able to give information on both attitudes and attainment, but I'm not convinced the secondary schools are willing to address that information, and plan on the basis of it.

Q: *Would using the Ladder at primary school be a way forward to ensure progression and, if so, which skills and levels?*

A: Some kind of consistency or standardization is really important because secondary schools are getting pupils from a really big number of feeder primaries who've all done different things, to different levels of complexity. So even if pupils have been learning, say, Spanish for three years, they might only have been doing interactive games on the whiteboard, or learnt various vocabulary topics. Other schools might have introduced reading and writing, and pupils might already be communicating with French pupils to quite a high level of competence. As far as I'm aware, the Languages Ladder does provide that kind of consistency, but I know there are financial issues for schools with this, and also it means pupils sitting even more tests. It's not so much a ladder of achievement or attainment we need, it's a curriculum we can all follow, so that all pupils follow the same route from Year 3 upwards. Obviously some will be more able than others, but it would give us a common pathway.

Q: *Have you observed/taught secondary language lessons and if so what did you learn?*

A: I have observed a secondary school lesson and it was useful as it showed me how much more enthusiastic younger pupils are and therefore why it is so important for primary-aged pupils to learn a foreign language. We have to work out how to sustain that enthusiasm.

Q: *What could secondary colleagues learn from observing primary language lessons?*

A: It is equally important for the secondary teachers to see how we approach the teaching and learning of foreign languages in the primary school and in particular the importance of oral work. Pupils are enjoying these lessons and not aware of the amount of learning they are doing!

Q: *What should primary and secondary language teachers be discussing?*

A: I think it is important that primary schools talk to their local secondary schools to discuss which languages are being taught at the primary and how the high schools will help pupils to progress once they start Year 7 rather than pupils becoming bored while other pupils learn the basics in a mixed ability class. I also think it is important for primary schools to be honest and if they don't have any language specialists on the staff, they should ask for help to ensure correct pronunciation and vocabulary, so that children don't learn things 'wrong' from the beginning.

Q: *What could you usefully plan together? Give a concrete example.*

A: We need to be sure that what we do at KS2 provides not only a good foundation for Key Stage 3, but good and useful language learning in itself so we need a common core.

Q: *Primary–secondary liaison seems to be problematic. Why do you think this is so and what might practical solutions be?*

A: Links between primary and secondary are historically poor. Primaries want to pass on information about pupils they have treasured for years and secondary schools want to learn for themselves and not have too many preconceived ideas before meeting the pupils. There is also a feeling of distrust almost between with both parties thinking they know best!! This means that often information that is passed on isn't always appreciated or used effectively! I do believe that in the case of languages we have to look to the secondary schools for help and advice and to lead the way as the majority of primaries don't have the specialist skills required for language learning.

## A secondary school languages teacher

Q: *How would you describe the sub-role of the primary–secondary liaison teacher within the HOD role?*

A: We have created a role within the department in charge of Community Links. The person i/c ideally will liaise with primary schools to gather information about prior primary MFL learning, languages that were taught, etc. In normal circumstances and bearing in mind that all primary schools should begin to teach MFL, the information should be given to secondary schools as a matter of normal procedure (just like English, Maths and Science). So it would be more a question of the HoD having access to primary school data that is given to secondary schools.

Q: *What primary languages information ideally would you like primary colleagues to pass on to the secondary school?*

A: (a) What languages have been taught, (b) For how long, (c) Content/SoW (ideally QCA), (d) Level achieved.

Q: *Would using the Ladder at primary school be useful to secondary teachers and, if so, which skills and levels?*

A: Yes, very. The new NC descriptors seem to tie in with the Ladder in terms of content and 'can do' statements. I would like to see all skills being covered. From previous experience I feel that primary school pupils can achieve the Breakthrough Levels 1–3 if not Preliminary 4–6, depending on ability. I feel that the understanding of how the Languages Ladder works is still very scatty at primary as well as secondary level.

Q: *Have you observed/taught primary language lessons and, if so, what did you learn? If not, how could such observation be useful?*

A: Yes, I have observed a Year 3 Spanish class and taught a Year 6 French class. Year 3 was very different in their learning. Writing skill was kept to a minimum whereas Year 6 French was basically a Year 7 lesson moved into Year 6. Colleagues who teach in primary schools have confirmed this and feel that Year 6 students are capable (and in many respects find it easier than Year 7) to retain vocabulary and structures normally offered in Year 7. Thus, progress in KS2 can be achieved.

Q: *What could primary colleagues learn from observing Yr 7 lessons?*

A: Language teaching strategy, the language itself. Classroom management in an environment where students have to listen, speak and be quiet almost at the same time.

Q: *What should primary and secondary colleagues be discussing in terms of primary–secondary liaison?*

A: Data/achievement/attainment need to be passed on. The role of the secondary schools needs to be redefined as the teaching in future has to come from primary schools rather than secondary schools. Ideally, there will be continuity in terms of languages offered or studied and of methodology and content.

Q: *What could you usefully plan together? Please give a concrete example.*

A: We are currently working out a timetable which will also result in some team teaching, the following week the primary school teacher teaches the planned lesson independently. – Week 1 Planning together + team teaching, Week 2 Primary teacher teaches independently, Week 3 Planning together + team teaching, Week 4 Primary teacher teaches independently, the idea is to offer two primary schools the same scheme, which would then work on a rotation basis. We are also planning to run weekly session in Spanish training and MFL teaching methodology. Partner primary schools are invited to attend (the LA has made money available for this). Again, this is to develop primary autonomy.

Q: *Primary–secondary liaison seems to be problematic. Why do you think this is so and what might practical solutions be?*

A: I think some of it is mentioned above. Primary school teachers have very little or no contact time. So taking on extra responsibility and regular training after school has proven to be problematic. Covering MFL lessons in primary schools through secondary teachers has proven to be costly and needs to be reduced. We see the next two years as a transition period dealing with issues, ideas, willingness, a plan, etc.

These teachers show a welcome willingness to not only talk but also to find ways to combat the perennial problems of e.g. time, logistics, funding and, with a new mindset, to engage in mutual learning. Big issues that need some agreement are the thorny issues of the place of writing and spelling, assessment opportunities and transfer data. Secondary teachers felt strongly that Yr 6 pupils need some introduction to the written word and spelling conventions, accents and connectives and that this meshes well with the work primary pupils do in literacy which sensitizes pupils to pattern and structure as well as to sentence and text levels. This can be done, as one teacher suggested, in a fun but challenging way with song words or in reading stories or poems. Secondary teachers, on whom the onus falls to respond to previous provision, can then better build on the ground covered so well in primary school and progress pupils' learning.

The results of the talking, sharing and learning can then become the basis of a transition plan for languages which we suggest all schools need in order to ensure progression and for sustainability of our still quite fragile subject. The statement in Box 7.1 reflects the commitment of a cluster of primary heads and secondary Heads of MFL. The commitment was drawn up after their first ever joint cross-phase meeting:

---

## Box 7.1 Joint commitment

Primary schools will . . .

- Summarize the experiences of their French curriculum and any relevant extra-curriculum provision.
- Pass transfer information to secondary schools about each pupil's experience, attainment and achievement in Languages as per details agreed. This is to be completed by mid-June and will form the basis of discussions when secondary Head of MFL visit primary Year 6 French teacher.

Secondary schools will . . .

- Be aware of the French curriculum experiences from their main feeder primary schools.
- Acknowledge the information they receive about the prior learning and the achievements of Y7 pupils in French.
- Act on the information received by using it to organize teaching groups.
- Act on the information received by providing differentiated provision.
- Adapt schemes of work taking into consideration prior learning in KS2.
- Secondary Head of MFL to meet with Year 6 Primary French teacher by mid-June and use information collected to inform organization of classes and planning for Year 7.

---

## A transition plan

In Chapter 6, we asserted the need for a transition plan to be part of the whole school languages policy. Below we suggest an outline of what that plan needs to include:

1   A statement that values cooperation and collaboration between primary and secondary colleagues and the benefits for teachers and pupils and details the expectations of such collaboration.

2   Arrangements for primary pupils visits to secondary school and induction into MFL at secondary school on those visits.

3   Arrangements for primary teachers to visit Yr 7 MFL secondary colleagues and for secondary teachers to visit Yr 6 primary colleagues to discuss teaching and learning and pupil assessment data and to undertake joint planning for transitional learning.

4   Details of coverage of topics, vocabulary, structures and skills at KS2 and in Yr 7 and an agreement on core coverage.

5   Assessment arrangements and agreement about transfer of useful data such as portfolio, 'can do' statements, tick lists, teacher comments, NC levels. Pupils should always take with them a record of achievement, as either a record of work in a folder or exercise book and/or an audio-recording.

6   A time frame for the plan.

7   The specification of transitional learning activities running through the end of Yr 6 into the early part of Yr 7.

Good ideas with respect to this last point include:

*Year 6*

- Sampling a lesson from a Yr 7 textbook.
- Enjoying a simple story, reciting and acting as the words are looked at to establish phoneme–grapheme correspondence.
- Simple spelling and basic grammar challenges (linking these to literacy).
- Learning to write a few sentences.
- Writing notices in the foreign language for around the classroom and school.
- Short emails to pen pals.
- Reading aloud or memorization competitions.

*Year 7*

- Devising challenge activities based on the Yr 7 textbook that clearly identifies primary coverage such as an interview scenario, a poem, a song.
- Formative integrated assessments in the form of quizzes in the early weeks to build up a picture of what the pupils know/do not know/do not know well, as part of the auditing procedure.
- Topic work that enables pupils to use what they know, e.g. create a brochure on their town or about a French town.
- Creating mini-plays in groups that require pupils to use previous as well as new learning.
- Skills lessons, e.g. vocabulary builders and pattern/grammar mind maps.

Such a plan provides a framework for primary and secondary subject leaders to work together to secure a framework for continuous and progressive learning and to contribute to the sustainability of cross-phase language provision in school. A plan keeps transition on the discussion agenda, makes expectations explicit and makes effective transition a reality.

## Activity

In small groups, consider the above transition plan and plan the outline of a series of transition lessons that go from Yr 6 summer term to the Autumn term of Yr 7. The idea is to prepare Yr 6 pupils for secondary stage learning and for Yr 7 pupils to experience consistency, consolidation as well as fresh challenge. What assessment data would be useful to follow the pupil? Present these ideas in your schools and get feedback about the feasibility of the learning plan.

## Making transition work: case studies

School cluster arrangements are now very common and are especially useful in providing a forum for both secondary and primary schools to work together. In one LA where transition generally was a major topic for the clusters, primary languages had been prioritized at one stage in recognition of its need for support as a new subject and its still rather fragile status. Teachers planned a transitional scheme of work together that began in the Spring term of Year 6 and continued in Year 7. It included selected topics that became the focus of explicit revision and planned progression, a project that the pupils started in Yr 6 and continued until half term at secondary school and reciprocal visits of teachers to classrooms with team teaching. It also included discussions with pupils in both Yr 6 and Yr 7 and invited their feedback.

Individual schools also sometimes take the lead as in the case of this secondary specialist school with training status. There is often an issue about how secondary schools can liaise with a large number of feeder primary schools. This is how one secondary school is going about developing transition arrangements in its area with over 30 feeder primary schools:

## Teachers talking: developing transition

My secondary school is going to introduce a training programme for partner primary schools from September onwards. The school currently teaches French and Spanish in Years 5 and 6 in two local primary schools. These lessons are taught by two different teachers. Primary school teaching therefore uses four of our lessons per week on the timetable. Lessons are solely taught by the secondary teacher. For the coming year, one secondary teacher will have a double lesson allocated a week to plan and team teach with their primary partner school A. The same will be repeated the following week with primary partner school B, whilst primary partner school A will base an independently taught lesson on the lesson plan devised the previous week. This rotation principle will hopefully allow primary schools to develop independence whilst finding support from subject specialists and working in collaboration. At the same time language lessons in Spanish and an introduction to the methodology of language teaching will be provided once a week for all primary schools in the borough. It is hoped that this new system will allow a large number of primary school teachers to find the linguistic confidence to teach the subject independently in future.

To some extent, all the primary schools benefit in this arrangement and it is to be hoped that other secondary schools in the cluster will work with their local primary schools too. It would also be beneficial for mutual teacher learning for primary colleagues to share leadership and their primary teaching expertise in the training programme.

## Activity

Arrange to spend a day at a secondary school observing language lessons across KS3 and KS4. Take a notebook with you – as you observe lessons and discuss issues with teachers, it will be useful for you to note not only curricular content across KS3 and KS4, but also particular teaching approaches, including skill and ability mix in teaching content. If the class teachers are happy for you to do so, work with pupils during small-group or pair activities – this will allow you to engage with the lesson content in a less remote way than merely observing from the back of the classroom, and also obviously to engage with pupils too.

Compile a short list of questions/discussion topics you may like to cover with languages staff – for example, how they approach transfer arrangements from a number of feeder primaries, how progression in language learning may be ensured, what strategies they advocate for assessment in Yrs 7 and 8 in particular, and to what extent they may be replicated at upper KS2. The issue of motivation at KS3 is particularly interesting – apparently prevalent across KS2, it seems to wane across KS3 – remember this is your chance to investigate and explore issues that interest you, and will inform your practice as primary languages teachers next year.

## Conclusion

Pupils frequently go from primary schools with a strong basis of learning to build upon. Some of this basis derives from effective formative experiences the pupils have had at primary school. To ensure a learning bridge, both primary and secondary teachers must commit themselves to certain agreed expectations. Both primary and secondary teachers, as well as their pupils, would benefit from transitional planning and, when they do visit each other, always enjoy being 'on the other side of the fence'. The support of the Headteacher in enabling this to take place is crucial. A degree of success in a child's cross-phase learning is dependent on successful transition so time must be found and a conversation prioritized to welcome and secure the new subject provision into mainstream transition arrangements and the curriculum. The conversation would give impetus for fresh learning and teaching. As one Year 7 lad put it: 'We have gone from bonjour to breakfast [at primary school]. And now we are doing about what we have for dinner.'

# 8 The role of the school-based subject mentor

This chapter discusses how to:

- create a framework for the development of the primary languages subject mentor
- establish a continuum of professional development for trainees across the training institution and training school
- observe trainees in the primary languages classroom and feedback effectively
- create a school-based mentorship framework.

## Introduction

Since 1993, with the publication of DFE 14/93 which advocated a more significant role for the primary school in the initial training of teachers, many schools and HEIs have entered into training partnerships which have increased the role and contribution of the school in the initial training of teachers. As partnership models have developed, the roles and responsibilities of both HEI- and school-based tutors and mentors have likewise evolved to provide a comprehensive framework of support for the trainee.

The introduction of languages into the primary curriculum has posed an organizational challenge for both sides of the partnership: the HEI must source tutors with relevant subject and pedagogical knowledge and experience in teaching languages to young learners, while the school should ideally provide trainees with opportunities to observe language lessons, and to gradually assume responsibility for the planning and delivery of them, as well as effective 'on-the-job' mentoring. Additionally, HEIs need to support the development of primary languages mentors. In 2003, a team of researchers from Liverpool Hope University recommended that: 'Schools need to develop effective mechanisms for supporting PMFL trainees and be supported in re-defining roles and responsibilities as necessary' (Rowe and Campbell 2005). It is, however, doubtful that this has been achieved in the intervening five years to date. The recent Ofsted report, *Primary Languages in Initial Teacher Training* found that:

> Many schools do not yet have specialist mentors for languages. Although trainees adapt the generic advice they are given well, they need specialist feedback on their teaching, for example, on how to use the foreign language more in lessons. In the best schemes, arrangements are made for external specialists to observe trainees teaching languages, while targeted training progressively

enhances the skills of mentors to support language teaching. School-based trainers value these early opportunities to develop their understanding of primary languages and want more. Mentors who have attended language courses offered by providers have often gone on to take advantage of further opportunities for professional development.

(2008: 5)

## Creating a framework for primary languages subject mentor development

Maynard defines the role of the school-based subject mentor as follows: 'to focus specifically on the development of student teachers/knowledge, understanding and skills in the teaching of one or several of the National Curriculum subject areas' (1997: 91). There is clearly a need then for a structured approach not only to the subject mentoring of primary languages trainees, but also in the development of the mentors themselves and it is in this context that the training institution has a significant role to play. Moyles and Stuart noted that:

> The areas of trainee competence most generally recognized within a range of background literature are as follows:
>
> - *Foundational studies in education*, such as knowledge based on curriculum subjects, learning and development, social and political context
> - *Generic teaching knowledge and skills,* such as general pedagogical knowledge, professional skills, teaching techniques and strategies
> - *Specialized pedagogical knowledge and skills,* such as subject or content to be taught, age group of learner, meeting individualized needs of learners and understanding pupils' backgrounds
> - *Field experiences,* such as teaching practice, observation of teaching, microteaching and assessment of teaching.
>
> (2003: 12)

Thus, it is not unreasonable to expect a mentor to be able to address each of these four areas effectively in their mentoring practice. In the context of primary languages, the latter two areas are of particular significance. Clearly, an effective *mentor* must also be an effective *practitioner* with the requisite subject knowledge and understanding of how to teach it. A three-tiered approach is necessary: first, the mentor must have an understanding of the role of the mentor *per se*; second, the mentor must have – or must acquire – an adequate baseline competence in the target language, and, third, should be provided with sufficient opportunity to observe and work with experienced practitioners in other schools, while gradually improving their own performance as a languages teacher in their own school. Both the school and trainees benefit from taking this approach: as the future mentor becomes more experienced in the languages classroom in preparation for the role of mentor, so the quality of the teaching and learning experience for the pupils is also enhanced.

Any training and development programme must take into account, and address, the needs of its target audience. Primary practitioners possess a wide variety of skills and it is important that the training institution understand these before designing the programme. Rowe and Campbell (2005) identified four possible profiles for primary languages subject mentors:

1    Experienced school-based tutor with PMFL expertise
2    Experienced school-based tutor with no PMFL expertise
3    New school-based tutor with PMFL expertise
4    New school-based tutor with no PMFL expertise.

Thus, the trainer should audit the current skills of potential languages mentors, and create a training programme accordingly, calling upon experienced non-subject-specific mentor trainers where necessary. To provide a more comprehensive training, a primary languages subject mentor training programme should be complemented by a discrete programme of needs-specific language training. Schools can contact their LA Primary Languages Adviser about the availability of these, or their training institutions, who may run language booster courses for trainees that are also suitable for in-service teachers.

## Teachers talking

### Assuming the role of primary languages subject mentor

An HEI tutor explains how she planned an initial programme of mentor training:

Q: *Does your school have a Primary Languages Subject Mentor?*

A: Yes, but the role is very much in development. As a school, we are actively involved in training new teachers, and as such, do have very experienced mentors on the staff. The challenge with languages is that while our mentors have a high level of both classroom experience and subject knowledge across the existing curriculum, this is simply not the case with languages. As Subject Leader, I'm currently assuming the role of mentor too, as I have a degree in French and Spanish, and it makes sense for me to assume the mentorship role too. I've been on various training courses in language teaching methodology for young learners, and have spent a lot of time with secondary colleagues, and observing them teaching our upper KS2 classes.

Q: *How do you define your role as Modern Languages Subject Mentor?*

A: First and foremost, the mentorship is important, then the subject. I see my role as supporting the development of new primary teachers, helping them understand how primary children respond to, and engage with, learning activities in the classroom. Mentors also have to be sure that trainees are sufficiently organized, and sufficiently aware of developments in the particular subject area, and that they are able to relate to the pupils in their care. I encourage them to think about subject knowledge, then to deconstruct it – just because we know something, and how to do something, doesn't mean we can automatically teach children how to do it – so that's a very important part of my role as mentor – looking very carefully at how trainees present and explain language, how they encourage pupils to use it, and how effective they are at recognizing pupils' understanding. This year, I've timetabled a weekly 30-minute feedback session, and I observe at least one language lesson a week.

Q: *To what extent do you think that primary practitioners are ready to take on this role?*

A: Well, overwhelmingly they're not. That's because many lack a secure subject knowledge base, and though they may well be experienced practitioners in general, and even understand approaches to teaching languages to young learners, the lack of subject knowledge does undermine their confidence. Gradually that should change though, as new teachers are coming through with an increased subject knowledge in at least one modern language.

Q: *In what ways does this role differ from that of the Modern Languages Subject Leader?*

A: The Subject Leader directs the whole-school vision for languages, and oversees progress on a school-wide basis. He or she is also responsible for staff training, and keeping staff abreast of new developments in the subject. There is likewise responsibility for secondary liaison. If two different members of staff have the subject leadership and mentoring roles, then clearly they would have to work closely together, because they are essentially both involved in training.

Q: *Does the same person necessarily have the same knowledge and skills to fulfil both roles?*

A: Not necessarily the same, no, but there is a lot of overlap. It's absolutely crucial that both keep up to date with the subject area, but, for example, the Subject Leader does not necessarily have to be an experienced mentor – there are a number of administrative responsibilities which go with the role of subject leader, which require a particular set of skills, which the mentor doesn't really call upon.

Q: *What role does the Modern Languages Subject Mentor play in the development of effective primary languages practitioners?*

A: Eventually the mentor will play a crucial role, but at the moment, mentorship of trainees in language teaching is very much underdeveloped. Trainees need to be able to observe experienced practitioners, so as primary teachers gain more experience in teaching languages, trainees will have increasing access to that. We do have secondary colleagues coming in on occasion and I always try to ensure that the trainees are able to observe them teaching, and we discuss issues arising from the observation as a small group.

Q: *How important is collaboration between the training institution and the school?*

A: Well, it's central to the success of the training programme, and that doesn't apply solely to languages. I do know people who see training as primarily the function of the institution, rather than the school, but the reality is that schools have to accept an increased and structured role in training.

Q: *What kind of training would you consider important for future Modern Languages Subject Mentors?*

A: Well, they've got to be able to speak the language. Perhaps not fluently, but certainly they require a level of mastery that goes beyond 'Bonjour!' They need to be able to adapt their language teaching practice in English to the teaching of a second language in a classroom setting – remember, all primary teachers already *are* language teachers to a greater or lesser extent. This should then be complemented by an understanding of what makes a good language lesson across the year groups. We shouldn't forget though that there are underlying skills in mentoring that are non-subject specific, such as being a good listener and observer, being able to engage a trainee in ongoing dialogue about performance and progress, being able to set reasonable targets and generally being committed to the role of mentor.

## Mentoring primary languages trainees during school experience: partnerships in action

An effective school-based languages teacher training programme depends largely on the communication and collaboration between the training institution and the school, and there are core elements which need to be addressed by both partners individually, as well as together.

### Prior to school placement

To facilitate both the professional development of trainees, the contribution of the trainees to pupils' language learning, and the enhancement of schools' languages programmes, the training institution tutor and the mentor together should ensure that:

- there is an outline of agreed competences against which to measure trainees' development;
- there is an agreed framework of progression for trainees' development;
- the trainee is fully aware of both the required competences and the framework of progression;
- if the trainee is following a languages Specialism, the assessment criteria are known and understood by all relevant parties;
- there is a timetable in place which allows trainees to observe, discuss, plan for learning, teach, experiment, reflect and evaluate;
- there are clear guidelines of how to support weaker trainees collaboratively;
- there are effective channels of communication within and between institution- and school-based tutors and mentors, as primary languages tutors and mentors may not necessarily have responsibility for training and development in other areas of the curriculum.

The training institution tutor needs to ensure that:

- Sufficient information is known about languages provision of each partnership or placement school before placing trainees. While a trainee on the generalist Primary PGCE programme may be adequately supported in their development in a school with a fairly unsophisticated language programme, this can limit their potential somewhat. A trainee on a Modern Languages Specialism does, however, need to be placed in a school where languages are embedded into the curriculum of the school, with sufficient opportunity for the trainee to both observe, and begin to teach. It may be necessary to conduct a simple audit of partnership or other placement schools to obtain this information in the current absence of a national database, as recommended by Rowe and Campbell (2005).
- The school is able to situate its contribution to training within the overall training programme. Thus, it needs comprehensive information about the campus-based training programme.
- The school understands at what stage of development as a primary languages practitioner the trainee is: a short tutorial before placement allows the tutor and trainee to identify current strengths and weaknesses, with areas for development. This information gives a baseline competence, and provides invaluable guidance for all parties throughout placement.
- The role and responsibilities of the primary languages mentor are clearly defined and agreed.
- A joint baseline observation with the subject mentor is timetabled in the first week of placement.
- A brief written report from the campus-based tutor to the languages mentor, with identified targets that the mentor can build on.

The mentor should ensure that:

- an observation schedule is in place;
- languages are embedded into the overall school-based training programme;
- there is sufficient time allowed for the trainee to teach languages without compromising other areas of their development as a primary practitioner;
- there is sufficient time in the trainee's timetable for discursive feedback;
- the trainee is aware of the school's languages policy;
- the trainee has a copy of both long- and medium-term planning (schemes of work) or an overview of the current languages programme;
- an understanding of what has been covered by individual year groups;
- access to plans of lessons already taught, including how homework may have been embedded into the homework timetable;
- access to available materials and resources;
- trainees have an awareness of pupils' progress in language learning;
- there are clear guidelines for trainees on how to monitor and record progress in language learning.

## During school placement

The training institution tutor and the mentor should ensure that:

- there is sufficient communication about trainees' ongoing progress, particularly where there may be cause for concern, which needs to be identified as soon as possible to allow for increased support and renewed target setting;
- the trainee continues to have sufficient opportunity to observe, discuss, teach;
- post-lesson evaluations are being completed;
- where the languages subject mentor is not the overall training mentor, that there is close liaison between the mentors. It is essential that the trainee's development as a languages teacher is aligned with his/her development as a primary practitioner as a whole;
- the school-based training plan is being managed effectively;
- there is a clear overview of trainees' ongoing development.

## On completion of placement

The training institution tutor and the mentor should ensure that:

- all relevant documentation and information is exchanged;
- any relevant targets for trainees' future development, including the Career Entry Development Profile (CEDP) have been identified.

# Observing the primary languages trainee

As Driscoll et al. (2004) point out:

> Teachers' knowledge is important. It encompasses knowledge about the language; subject- and age-specific teaching methods; resources; the curriculum; the children as individuals and their learning needs. These aspects need to be included in initial teacher training ... Specialist teachers may be more fluent, but primary teachers have the advantage of knowing the school and pupils better.

Thus, it is important that the language specialist and the primary practitioner share each other's expertise to exploit fully the range of knowledge, understanding and experience that they have between them. It is equally important that they, acting as training institution tutor and school-based mentor, have a shared understanding of what a 'good' primary languages lesson is (see Chapters 1 and 2), and as suggested above, this should be a key feature of any mentor training programme offered by the institution. This is not to say that trainees will not learn from the inevitable mistakes, unexpected outcomes and general problems that are an inherent part of the teaching and learning process; on the contrary, this is rich terrain for teacher discussion and learning.

In terms of both quality assurance, and consistency of approach and trainee support, it is good practice to ensure that lessons are observed in a systematic way by all parties, following the same observation template. The tutor, mentor and trainee then have a common platform for discussion and dialogue, and it facilitates the tracking of trainee progress, the setting of progressive targets, and the ability to identify which targets have or have not been met, and thus what steps may be taken by the trainee to do so.

Ideally, a placement of seven weeks should accommodate at least four observations of a languages lesson. The first observation should be jointly conducted by the tutor and mentor, and allow for a post-observation 30-minute tutor/mentor discussion session, followed by a 30-minute discursive feedback session with the trainee. Keeping a record of the main outcomes of each observation provides a useful summary of trainee input and progress and a copy filed by both mentor and trainee.

Before the observation, consider the following:

- where you should sit – consider carefully whether you will be able to observe sufficiently well from that vantage point;
- will you be a participant observer (for example, acting as TA), or a completely neutral observer?
- will you set a particular focus for this observation in prior agreement with the trainee? For example, the use of the target language when managing behaviour; encouraging pupils to engage with the written word; promoting speaking skills.

# The role of feedback in supporting trainees' professional development

Feeding back to trainees after observation is an integral part of the development process. Discursive feedback, i.e. where mentor and trainee engage in a reciprocal discussion about a lesson, what Maynard calls 'a learning conversation', can encourage trainees to be more reflective and analytical, and to approach an observation not as a 'test' but as an opportunity to learn with and from a more experienced practitioner. The process of 'feeding forward', i.e. setting negotiated and agreed targets, serves likewise to engage the trainee more proactively and reflectively in the process.

A feedback session can be structured as follows:

- Ask the trainee whether he/she thinks the lesson was a success, with particular reference to the learning objectives, explaining why.
- Encourage the trainee to articulate their thoughts on a particular strength and a possible weakness in the lesson.
- To what extent did learning take place, and what is the evidence for this?
- If a particular focus has been agreed for this observation, ask the trainee to evaluate how effective their input was.
- Ask the trainee to suggest ways that the strengths might be built upon, and the weaknesses addressed.
- Looking closely at the lesson plan, ask the trainee to explain the rationale for the lesson, then discuss whether this rationale is reasonable within the medium- or longer-term plan.
- Discuss the range of teaching and learning activities and consider together how effective these were.
- Ask the trainee what points they might include in the post-lesson evaluation – do you agree these are reasonable?
- Discuss the implications of the evaluation for the following lesson – how might this inform planning?

Review sessions are a useful tool also: a mid-placement review allows both mentor and trainee to assess whether targets are being met, and what might need to be done to ensure that they will be by the end of placement.

---

## Activity

Read the following observation report written by an experienced primary languages mentor. In small groups, discuss:

- how you would approach the oral feedback session based on the report;
- what you consider to be the strengths/weaknesses of the report.

# Lesson Observation Proforma

**Name**
Matt Bell

**Date**
10.05.08

**Tutor/Mentor**
Pauline Scott (Mentor)

**School**
Hill Crest Primary

**Subject/Topic**
Mon école

**Group/Number in group**
Year 5/21

## Key Strengths of Lesson Planning

Your plan was again sufficiently detailed, with an LO: To say seven things I have – clearly you are encouraging pupils to build more complex phrases, and use the language they are learning. You planned to introduce seven pencil case items, and combine the vocabulary items with the structure 'j'ai'. You also used these items to highlight the difference in genders in French – a very painless way of doing it I thought, and one that the pupils subsequently responded to extremely well. Do remember to keep going over this during the course of the next few lessons – I think by the end of the 45 minutes it was evident that a fair number of pupils had not sufficiently embedded either the vocabulary, their genders, or the distinction between 'un' and 'une'. You are providing pupils with meaningful and interesting opportunities to develop their oracy skills – so good cross-curricular thinking – and you canvas their thoughts and opinions, encouraging them to think about what they already know, in a really effective way – lots of hands waving in the air – always a very good sign!

In general, I might be inclined to think of multiple LOs – more in terms of: to begin to learn seven common pencil case objects; to discuss the notion of gender in French; to recognize the difference between 'un' and 'une' and to begin to formulate sentences describing what they have using the structure 'j'ai' – this gives a more comprehensive picture of what you – and they – were actually doing – what do you think?

Your plan notes in writing, rather than typescript, 'set homework' – I didn't note that you set any homework – was that intentional, or because you ran out of time? If you are setting homework, I'd draw the final learning activity to a close perhaps 10 minutes before lesson end, including time to tidy up, which gives you lots of time to explain the homework – younger pupils often need very clear, very precise guidance and instructions. In future, could you also specify what the homework actually is – this will help you plan future lessons, monitor progress, and is a useful record for both you and the class teacher. I think your explicit inclusion of the Framework objectives is a useful planning strategy, and it will enable you to map out longer-term objectives, and keep track of progress.

## Standards

Q22 plan for progression across the age and ability range
Q23 design opportunities for learners to develop their literacy, numeracy and ICT

Q24 plan homework to sustain and consolidate
Q29 evaluate the impact of their teaching and modify classroom practice where necessary

## Teaching

What a flying start – brilliant! Everyone engaged and absolutely absorbed in your lesson. After our discussion last time, I kept a keen eye on the clock – and I thought you brought the initial whole-group oral activity to an end right on time – 15 minutes is definitely the limit for this class.

You use the TL to excellent effect, lots of it, but with English where you feel it necessary – we can perhaps now think more in terms of how to maximize pupil use of the TL? Perhaps start off the lesson with general conversational gambits that they can engage in – greetings, how are you, what's the day and date today (followed by a volunteer writing that on the board), what's the weather like today (they should be experts on that by now!) – perhaps a bonus of some kind for those who can ask and answer three questions – encourage them to ask each other too, not just you!

You encourage pupils to use their knowledge of English to decode French, as well as to make links between the sound of a word and its written form. I think this works extremely well. Again, you use a range of strategies, such as mime, gesture, finger writing and chant to help pupils learn. I noted that your facial expressions are working wonders in terms of managing behaviour – several times I saw pupils respond to your 'look' – well done!

The group is lively, and as Claire has pointed out, do find it hard to work together for protracted periods of time. Behaviour did start to become sloppy, and I might have moved on to a worksheet exercise after the whole-group oral activity – something like match the picture with the word, with extension activities along the lines of word gaps (for spelling) and sentence gaps (for the beginning stages of working at sentence level) – this I think would have calmed them down somewhat. Although you moved on to a different activity after the whole-group starter, it was in effect another whole-group one – I felt that the pace of the lesson slumped somewhat during the distribution of the – once again – lovely picture resources, and the slump was filled by an increase in their liveliness! This meant that the Q&A with Qui a? J'ai . . . was somewhat less effective than the opening activity.

I wonder if you can think of ways to get you away from the front of the class, and moving around, so that you are regularly literally close to each and every pupil? Your WB resources are fantastic, but they do mean that you are 'glued' to the laptop – so, perhaps you could either move the laptop, or designate a 'laptop' monitor on a rota basis, or not include so many WB-driven activities? That's the key question when we use ICT – is it supporting learning effectively? At the point where we question if sound learning is going on simply because we are obliged to operate the technology, then that's where we should consider alternative strategies – would you agree?

## Standards

Q10a knowledge of a range of teaching, learning, behaviour management skills
Q10b personalize learning and provide opportunities for all learners

Q17 know how to use skills in literacy, numeracy and ICT to support their teaching
Q18 understand how children and young people develop
Q19 know how to identify and support children whose progress is affected by change
Q25 teach lessons across the age and ability range
Q25a use a range of teaching strategies and resources
Q25b build on prior knowledge
Q25c adapt language to suit the learner
Q25d demonstrate the ability to manage learning

### Assessing, Monitoring and Giving Feedback

You praise the children very well, and they thoroughly appreciate that praise – you kept a good eye on the class, and were able to reward consistently good behaviour with stickers – exactly where they were due. You correct errors and misunderstandings in a way that is non-threatening, and certainly not demotivating. As noted in my previous report, you would find it useful to being to adopt a more structured approach to formative assessment, and include some simple AfL strategies. Are you now able to record formative notes on pupils' progress? Do you get opportunity to discuss progress with Claire, and to get a picture of their general progress across the curriculum? An understanding of where each child is in his or her learning can greatly inform your own planning and teaching.

### Standards

Q11 know the assessment requirements
Q12 know a range of approaches to assessment
Q26a make effective use of assessment and monitoring
Q26b assess learning needs in order to set challenging objectives
Q27 provide constructive feedback
Q28 guide learning to reflect on their learning

### Learning Environment, Teamwork and Collaboration

Again, your warmth and enthusiasm were very much in evidence. You have a good working relationship with the class teacher, and you thoroughly look part of the school team from the moment you walk into school. I'd say the pupils are responding increasingly well to you, and are accepting you more in the role of 'authority' – clearly, they are keen to work for you and with you.

### Standards

Q4 communicate effectively
Q5 recognize and respect the contribution of colleagues
Q6 commitment to collaborative working
Q30 establish purposeful and safe learning environment
Q31 Clear Framework for classroom discipline
Q33 ensure work colleagues are appropriately involved

### Relationships with Children and Young People
You manage behaviour well, though when the group start to get a little over-lively, you tend to insist on silence before you continue, and the longer you wait, the more unlikely silence becomes, as those who have indeed been silent are now also getting rather fidgety – as we've discussed before, there are times when silence is not necessarily the best thing to ask for – and waiting for it can impact quite negatively upon the flow and feel of the lesson. If you keep the pace up, moving swiftly on, keeping pupils occupied and challenging them effectively, the level of noise and misbehaviour tends not to rise quite so dramatically – if we look at what compromised pace in this lesson, I'd summarize it as too much whole-group oral work, with no 'calming-down' activities in between, too much time spent over distributing resources, and too much 'leading from the front' – what do you think? Try to reduce those elements, and see to what extent that is able to keep the pace up, and the pupils occupied.

### Standards
Q1 high expectations, commitment to ensuring full educational potential
Q2 demonstrate positive values, attitudes and behaviour

### Professional Knowledge and Understanding
I would say you have an excellent understanding of language and teaching strategies appropriate to this year group, and as you become more familiar with the group, you are becoming increasingly adept at planning activities and applying strategies that work well. You listen to other people's ideas, and use them where appropriate – that is not to say that you do not have a wealth of really good ideas yourself! You are building up an impressive bank of teaching ideas and resources, and improving your overall performance in the classroom with tenacity, commitment and style!

### Standards
Q3a be aware of professional duties
Q3 be aware of the policies and practices of the workplace
Q7 reflect on and improve practice
Q8 have a creative and critical approach to innovation
Q9 act upon advice
Q14 secure knowledge of the subject and pedagogy
Q15 understand non and statutory curricula and frameworks
Q21a be aware of legal requirements re the promotion of the well-being of children

### Key Strengths of Lesson
Again, resources! Planning – you're really thinking about things, even if this is not quite so explicit on the plan itself, it shows in the teaching.
   Your desire to challenge the pupils.

---

**Targets arising out of this lesson**

1    Think about when to introduce 'calming' activities, i.e. move away from
     whole-group work, and look at how you can 'free' yourself from the WB,
     enabling you to move around the room more.
2    You're using the framework to good effect, please do continue! Start now to
     adopt a more structured approach to assessing and recording progress (talk to
     the class teacher about this too – what strategies does she employ that you may
     be able to replicate? What kinds of info would she find most useful?)
3    Have you set a date for giving a short presentation to staff at a staff meeting
     about your work?

---

Tutors/mentors need to ensure that:

- there is timely submission of the written observation template to each other, and to the trainee;
- there is sufficient time to allow for oral feedback as soon as possible after the lesson;
- the trainee is given adequate opportunity to discuss his/her reflections and observations about the lesson;
- there is a clear framework to the feedback sessions.

The example is a particularly detailed one designed to give the fullest picture to the reader. It is, however, important to note that some observation feedback will be shorter or written in some form of teacher shorthand. What underlies good practice is that common observation criteria are followed by all observers as a basis for learning or discursive feedback and that the trainee is able to engage in the process in order to understand what has worked well and why, and what can be improved and how.

## Conclusion

The role of the subject mentor cannot be over-emphasized in establishing and sustaining effective early language teaching and learning in a series of 'learning conversations'. While the generally inexperienced trainee is in essence mentored by the more experienced colleague, the real satisfaction in the mentoring process is to be gained in the dialogue that takes place and the mutual learning that derives from this dialogue. There is always something worthwhile to be learnt from the fresh new ideas of the trainees as well as from the hand of experience. This partnership of minds then goes beyond attention to the framework and tracking through the competences, important though these are, and extends to the co-construction of knowledge in the subject field.

# 9 In the field

## From theory to practice

---

This chapter discusses how to:

- prepare for school experience
- gather relevant information about the primary languages programmes in schools
- engage with the concept of the reflective practitioner and its role in the professional development of teachers
- write a reflective school experience journal
- observe and reflect on primary language teachers at work
- identify features of best practice in the primary languages classroom.

---

## Introduction

Being in school, and working as part of the school team, is integral to any programme of teacher training. Throughout your initial year, you will spend increasing amounts of time in school, with increasing amounts of responsibility for teaching and learning across the curriculum. In terms of languages programmes in schools, you may well find that there are a number of significant differences in the way that languages are delivered, and comparing provision across schools will give you a valuable insight into how effective languages programmes may be structured.

## Preparing for school experience: knowing your school

It is always good practice to inform yourself as much as possible about the school, and its vision, before you begin your placement. Some training programmes schedule pre-placement orientation and observation and opportunities to meet with mentors, but there is much you can do independently:

- Read the most recent Ofsted report (www.Ofsted.gov.uk) – this will give you a detailed overview of the school's strengths, and any identified areas for improvement. Look for information about the range of languages spoken within the school community. Increasingly, languages programmes are being included in primary inspection reports, so look particularly for any specific mention of languages provision, noting commendations or recommendations.

- Read the school's website carefully, noting information about the curriculum as a whole, the language(s) being taught, and any extra-curricular activities – many schools offer languages programmes in the form of after-school clubs which you may be able to contribute to.
- If this is your second placement, investigate whether any of your co-trainees have already undertaken a placement there and ask them about the language programme.

## Being organized

Organizing and managing both time and workload effectively is a key professional attribute and one which you need to acquire during your training. To ensure that you get the most from your time in school, before you begin your placement, you should:

- create a Primary Languages file with clearly labelled sections
  - TEACHING: your own lesson plans, teacher lesson plans, medium- and longer-term SoW
  - CLASSROOM OBSERVATION: reports on your lessons by mentors/tutors, and the reports you write during observation of class teachers
  - RESOURCES: teaching resources and worksheets
  - ASSESSMENT: school assessment policy, language assessment policy, assessment/recording frameworks, information on pupil attainment
  - PUPIL WORK: examples of pupil work
  - POLICY DOCUMENTS: to include a copy of the school SIP and ML policy, and other relevant documentation such as the role specification for the ML Subject Leader
  - REFLECTION AND EVALUATION: reflective notes;
- draw up a list of the kinds of data about primary languages you wish to gather during placement;
- map your time carefully against your data targets, regularly noting each piece of information in writing – this will help you identify where there are gaps in your data.

## Languages in the primary school: understanding logistics and practicalities

The logistics and practicalities of including languages in the primary curriculum can be complex, and it is important that you gain a comprehensive understanding of the organizational and strategic issues that schools may face. Remember that each school has its own set of immediate priorities and longer-term goals, and it is entirely possible that languages may not yet feature prominently in its SIP.

Ensure you have a notebook with you to write your observations and comments, and use the following points as a preliminary guide:

## Subject leadership

- Is there a Languages Subject Leader? How was this responsibility allocated?
- What are the key responsibilities of the Languages subject leadership role?
- Does the school have a Languages policy as part of the School Improvement Plan (SIP)?
- Who directs that policy, and what is included in it?

## Features of the languages programme

- To what extent are languages embedded into the curriculum?
- What language/s is/are taught? What has driven this choice?
- What year groups receive language lessons? How has this been decided?
- Are any pupils disapplied from modern languages? Why?
- Do the languages lessons get 'moved about' or cancelled more than other subjects, for example, for museum trips, rehearsing for assembly/Christmas play/other school events?
- Is there a local Specialist Language College (SLC)? If so, what is the extent of its involvement in the primary languages programme?
- What is the perceived role of the Local Authority (LA) Languages Adviser?
- How does the school manage transition arrangements to Year 7?

## Teaching and learning

- Who delivers the lessons? Why has that particular model of delivery been adopted?
- What length are the lessons?
- Do you see evidence of the application of the KS2 Framework for Languages in planning?
- Is provision made for EAL/SEN?
- What resources does the school use and to what effect?
- Are learning objectives clearly defined?
- Are there cross-curricular approaches to language teaching?
- Are there clear links to literacy and other skills, such as ICT, in language teaching?
- To what extent is intercultural awareness embedded in T&L?

## Assessment

- To what extent is assessment embedded into language teaching?
- What formative or summative assessment strategies are employed?
- Do teachers systematically record pupil progress?
- Are there elements of self- and peer assessment?

### Subject knowledge

- Do staff members appear confident in their language skills and thus ability to teach languages?
- Do staff members have knowledge and understanding of the KS2 Framework for Languages and the KS3 Framework for Languages?

### Attitudes to language teaching and learning

- What is the range of pupil languages in the school?
- What do the pupils think about languages and language lessons?
- Do all staff members support the inclusion of languages into the curriculum? Why/why not?
- Do parents and governors support the inclusion of languages? Is their support important?
- Can you evaluate the priority of languages in your school? How have you reached this evaluation?

### Training and professional development

- What kind of training is available to staff, and how effective is it?
- How do staff characterize their development needs? For example, language upskilling, language teaching methodology, assessment strategies.

Map out your data collection across the placement period in the form of a diary, also noting how you will collect data, for example, a scheduled meeting with the Languages Subject Leader, attendance at a staff meeting or training event.

## The reflective practitioner: improving practice through critical enquiry

### Learning through reflection

For many educational and organizational theorists, reflection on practice is fundamental to professional development. But how do we do it? How do we ensure that our thinking goes beyond the surface level onto a deep – and therefore *critical* level? John Dewey (1933) suggests the following:

> One can think reflectively only when one is willing to endure suspense and to undergo the trouble of searching. To many persons both suspense of judgement and intellectual search are disagreeable; they want to get them ended as soon as possible. They cultivate an over-positive and dogmatic habit

of mind, or feel perhaps that a condition of doubt will be regarded as evidence of mental inferiority. It is at the point where examination and test enter into investigation that the difference between reflective thought and bad thinking comes in.

For Dewey, reflective thinking is 'active, persistent, and careful consideration' of one's own beliefs and knowledge, involving a 'willingness to engage in constant self-appraisal and development'.

Donald Schön (1983) explored and developed the concept of reflection further. For him, reflection *in* action – that is, *during* the event or encounter, as opposed to reflection *on* action, that is, *after* the event or encounter has taken place, lies at the very heart of true reflection. Schön was concerned with *professional practice* as a whole and there are clear parallels of practice across the professional spectrum. Schön also emphasizes the use of 'judgement'. Professional judgement – and the appropriate application of it – are a key skill in the teacher's repertoire. Schön's notion of 'professionalism' resonates with that of Lawrence Stenhouse (1975) who summarized the 'critical characteristics' of what he terms 'extended professionalism' as follows:

- the commitment to systematic questioning of one's own teaching as a basis for development;
- the commitment and the skills to study one's own teaching;
- the concern to question and to test theory in practice by the use of those skills.

In summary, true reflection requires an openness and honesty, a commitment to 'critical self-enquiry' (Holly 1989), and the willingness to adapt practice according to the results of that self-enquiry.

## Reflective approaches to school experience

Understanding how schools are managing the inclusion of languages into the curriculum, and in what ways teachers are developing their practice to enable them to teach languages effectively, is not only a 'fact-finding' exercise – it serves to inform our understanding of what constitutes best practice. Similarly, when we observe teachers at work, or are observed ourselves, the real purpose is to deepen our understanding of what elements of our practice support learning most effectively, and what we might do to improve those elements which can be identified as less effective. Thus, teachers are simultaneously *learners,* and that is the heart of reflective practice. Remember that 'critical' is not of itself 'negative' – its sense lies more in being constructive – understanding how we ourselves learn, gaining insight into the rationale for, and the consequences of, our decisions and actions, and engaging in 'critical self-enquiry', influences and informs our practice as teachers. Consequently, both observation and practice must always be accompanied by critical reflection.

## Activity

Discuss in small groups the comments made by two primary teachers. Are the points they make relevant and reasonable? To what extent do you agree with their observations on reflective practice, and why? How would you characterize your own approach to reflective practice?

**Teacher 1:** Well, of course, I always think about what has happened in school. It's pretty unavoidable really. Actually, most teachers are probably doing it without calling it 'reflective practice'. I do know that if things have gone well, and the pupils have enjoyed the lesson, I go home feeling really good. That makes me feel that I have done things right. I try and analyse what it is I've done right, and usually it's the kind of activities that I've used – the pupils love to be allowed to talk and express their opinions. If I vary the activities I know I can keep their attention. I have to say I rarely reflect *in* action. In fact, I don't think I ever do – how can you do that and still keep the lesson under control? At the end of the day, I've got a whole syllabus to get through, and I plan my lessons around that syllabus, so regardless of how things might be going in a particular lesson, I have to make sure I get through my plan. If I don't get through the syllabus, everyone would complain wouldn't they? Later on, I might change that particular lesson for another class, but I can't actually think of a time when I've done that. As a teacher you have to accept that some lessons simply don't go as well as others.

**Teacher 2:** We've always been encouraged to reflect on our practice here – in fact, I think it's generally accepted to be essential to good practice and ongoing 'quality control'. I quite like the idea of 'reflection-in-practice' – if you sense that the way you are teaching something is turning the children off in some way, or is simply not getting through to them, then I think you should respond to that immediately really – it's not easy – maybe it gets easier with practice – but I'd rather do that than suffer a whole lesson where everyone just feels frustrated and bored. That's my worse nightmare actually – because the standard of behaviour drops quite dramatically when the pupils are not engaged. Of course, what you decide to do might not go down very well either – but doesn't practice make perfect?

## The reflective school experience journal

The value of reflective journals as an integral part of the professional learning process is becoming increasingly recognized. Dart et al. (1998) noted how their students became more able to recognize the links between theory and practice while Heath (1998) encouraged the use of what he terms 'double entry' journals to encourage students to revisit initial reflections, essentially enhancing the reflective learning process. At its most basic, a journal allows you to note anything you consider important or interesting during your time in school. You may find that as you begin your journal, your observations are predominantly descriptive, rather than analytical. As you write, keep the following features of an effective reflective journal in mind:

- The journal acts as a repository for reflections on current professional practice, your own, and that of the teachers you work with.
- The journal is a record of reflections and observations you will be able to call upon to contribute to iterative professional development.
- The journal enables you to reflect upon and analyse your progress, and provides a timeline and record of learning.
- The journal enables you to identify changes in practice, and to evaluate the *how?* and the *why?* – not just simply the *what?* This is integral to reflecting on practice.

Remember that while journals are about thinking, they are equally about writing, the relationship between the two and how they contribute as a whole to the learning process. As you read through your journal at regular intervals, reflect also upon the nature of your writing – you may favour a 'formal' approach, or you may prefer a more 'stream of consciousness' approach. You may prefer to write your journal by hand, or to word-process your handwritten notes at a later stage – this would replicate somewhat Heath's notion of 'double entry journals' – it may be that as you write up your initial reflections, you have other interpretations, or reach slightly different conclusions than you did at first. Sometimes you might prefer to draw pictures, make diagrams, or create mind-maps. Whichever approach you take, is it supporting your reflection, and therefore your learning, effectively?

The reflective school experience journal must go beyond the merely descriptive, and consider the implications of classroom practice for pupil learning. All observations and conclusions are explained, and alternative approaches are suggested. The following is an extract from a reflective journal by a trainee, Simon, on a Modern Languages Specialism. Here, he reflects on what he considers to be effective practice in language teaching, considering issues surrounding the optimal age for introducing languages, the use of the target language in the classroom, the blend of the four skills in language lessons, and whether appropriate challenges are being set for pupils:

## Trainees reflecting

I find that, in general, the younger children are, the more enthusiastic they are to learn and embrace new ideas. Why not teach children the target language when they are most likely to be influenced and inspired? After observing three Year 5 language classes during the week one thing immediately becomes clear. The teacher attempts to include all four skills; speaking and listening; writing; reading to at least some extent in every lesson. As with the majority of subjects at this particular primary school, the curriculum is adhered to through working through activities in a textbook. The emphasis, however, is definitely on speaking and listening. At the start of every lesson the teacher spends a minimum of three minutes communicating with pupils in the target language through a simple question and answer session which is often linked to the current topic of work. 'What is the day today? What do you do at the weekend?', etc. I find this to be an effective start to a language lesson as it engages the pupils immediately, honing their speaking and listening skills whilst also recapping on previous work. Listening comprehension is also a common feature of all three language lessons. The teacher plays audio relating to the topic in hand and at various points asks questions in the target language to check children's understanding. In this way children practise their listening skills through hearing a native speaker, and both their listening and speaking capacities through understanding and responding to the questions posed by the teacher. At least 75% of each lesson this week is devoted to speaking and listening. Writing generally occurs in the last 10–15 minutes of each lesson with activities completed from the textbook such as matching beginning and endings of sentences or filling in missing adjectives from word banks. Reading is practised (albeit sparingly) through reading aloud of activity instructions, questions and passages which form the listening comprehension. On reflection I do feel that the emphasis on speaking and listening constitutes effective practice. After all, reading and writing skills cannot be developed until speaking (particularly) and listening skills have been at least fundamentally acquired. I would, though, like to see more taxing writing activities. Matching and copying out parts of sentences together with word bank activities do indeed reinforce vocabulary and sentence structure. However, on the teacher's own admission, this Year 5 class are extremely talented and in my opinion could easily develop their own sentences. I shall be interested to see if this independent writing opportunity occurs in future language lessons.

Focusing on the value of homework to embed classroom language learning, Simon notes:

According to the head teacher, homework is considered to be an integral part of the school ethos. It consolidates and enhances learning, promotes independence and allows parents and carers to see the level of their child and what they are studying. Children should receive a maximum of one hour homework per day. At Year 2, however, the homework issued is considerably less than this, perhaps understandably for children of a younger age. From general observation it appears that many homework activities involve writing particularly in the Year 5 language lessons where completing a writing activity for homework is seen to build upon the speaking and listening activities which form the central part of each lesson. Homework is then particularly important as it ensures a balance between the four language skills.

If you are interested in exploring reflective practice further, an excellent online starting point is: www.rtweb.info.

## Primary language teachers at work: observing good practice

One of the key strategies for identifying the features of good teaching practice is the observation of experienced practitioners at work. During school experience, you should aim to observe as many languages lessons as possible, in a range of year groups. In classroom observation, it's often tempting to try to observe 'everything', rather than targeting the specific areas you wish to focus on. Before you observe a lesson, ask for a copy of the scheme of work and the lesson plan as these will inform your understanding and evaluation of the lesson. Figure 9.1 is an example of a lesson observation exercise from a Year 5 French group.

| Year Group......... | Date/Time ............. | Teacher.................. |
|---|---|---|
| **Focus** | **Observation Target** | **Comments** |
| **Physical environment** | Do the language lessons take place in the pupils' normal classroom, or elsewhere? | *Yes, normal classroom – they do move into PE hall occasionally* |
| | Can all pupils clearly see the WB at all times? | *No, some pupils actually sit with their backs to the WB, and a number 'gave up' turning round to look at it* |
| | Does the classroom have a languages display? | *Yes, a small one – it's a 'work in progress'* |
| | Who creates that display, and what kind of content is included? (For example, are there visual prompts for classroom instructions in the target language? Do pupils contribute to the display and to what extent?) | *Very much an evolving process – pupils contribute to the display as integral part of learning process* |
| | Is the display working as a learning tool? | *Yes, a collaborative effort with class teacher* |

**Figure 9.1** An example of a lesson observation exercise from a Year 5 French group

| Year Group......... | Date/Time .............. | Teacher................... |
|---|---|---|

| Focus | Observation Target | Comments |
|---|---|---|
| | How are the pupils seated during languages lessons? | *On their normal grouped tables* |
| | Does the seating arrangement lend itself to a communicative approach to teaching and learning? | *To small-group and pair work, yes but not whole-group as they're all facing different ways – also quite difficult to move around physically so they tend to stay at their tables – not sure that the ability mix works well* |
| | Does it facilitate whole-group, small-group and pair work? | |
| **Planning** | Is the teacher working from a SoW? | *No structured SoW in place yet* |
| | Are the learning objectives and outcomes clearly defined in the lesson plan? | *Yes, Oracy 5.1, Literacy 5.2* |
| | Are key structures and language detailed? | *No, I wasn't sure which particular structures were being worked on* |
| | Are differentiation strategies clear? | *Not really – reading/writing texts could easily have been differentiated; teacher expected similar oral responses too* |
| **Teaching and Learning** | Does the teacher explain objectives/outcomes to the pupils? | *Yes, they knew what the lesson was going to be about* |
| | Do the pupils appear to understand what they are doing and why? | *They did at the beginning, but started to get confused at the writing activity* |
| | Does the lesson start with a recap of the preceding lesson? | *Yes, it went on for ages, not many pupils seem to retain much* |
| | Did the teacher use a starter activity and to what effect? | *The recap seemed to be the starter, then straight into working with texts could use more, particularly praise and other instructions; pupil use very limited* |
| | How much target language is used by the teacher and pupils, and to what effect? | |
| | Does the teacher use the target language to manage behaviour? | *Not really, though some instructions etc could easily be in French quite interactive* |
| | How interactive is the lesson? | *Teacher didn't lead too much* |

**Figure 9.1**   (*Continued*)

| Year Group......... | Date/Time .............. | Teacher.................... |
|---|---|---|

| **Focus** | **Observation Target** | **Comments** |
|---|---|---|
| | Does the teacher move around? Do the pupils? Why and when? | *Pupils stayed at their tables mostly, teacher at the WB – the writing activity would have benefited from teacher moving around groups* |
| | Are opportunities for pupil engagement with language learning maximized? | *Could use more TL, and more exposure to short, manageable chunks of written language* |
| | Do you see evidence that pupils are producing language themselves, rather than simply responding to learned prompts? | *No, at this stage, they seem perplexed by anything other than 'known' language in exactly the way they're used to hearing it* |
| | How does the teacher work on pronunciation? | *Teacher models good pronunciation* |
| | Is there a blend of the four skills, or an emphasis on speaking and listening for example? | *Blend of four skills, too much emphasis on reading/writing at this stage – volume too much* |
| | Does the teacher adopt a variety of teaching approaches to address a range of learner strategies? | *Yes, though mainly audio approaches* |
| | Does the teacher use mime, gesture, facial expression as both a teaching strategy and a means of communication? | *Mostly, but often resorts to using English orally instead* |
| | To what extent can you see a cross-curricular approach to language teaching? | *French taught by class teachers, within the 45-minute lesson timeframe, so no real evidence of integrating other subjects at the moment* |
| | Do the lessons focus on 'language' or a blend of language, learning about language, and cultural input? | *No cultural input – the reading/ writing texts could have had an intercultural focus* |
| | Are literacy and numeracy skills being reinforced through the medium of the target language? | *Literacy yes, but in unmanageable chunks* |
| | How much comparison with English is embedded into the lesson? For example, looking at cognates, or comparing phonetics? | *Some comparison with English which pupils found interesting* |

**Figure 9.1**   (*Continued*)

| Year Group......... | Date/Time .............. | Teacher................... |
|---|---|---|

| Focus | Observation Target | Comments |
|---|---|---|
| | How is new language presented, then practised? | *No new language presented today, lots of practice of previously covered language in terms of learning new language, not sure* |
| | Are Q&A techniques used to good effect? | *Lots of Q&A in English, but not in TL* |
| | How do pupils note new vocabulary? | *They have no formal way of recording vocabulary or structures* |
| | Are activities varied, and do they involve whole/small-group, pair and individual work? | *Yes, good mix, but some go on too long* |
| | How does the teacher manage that variety? | *Explains at beginning what the class will be doing, has all resources to hand and keeps up good pace* |
| | Are songs, rhymes and games used in the language lessons? To what extent? Are these used effectively as learning tools? How? | *Didn't see any games – a games starter or as part of the plenary would have worked well* |
| | Are the activities reasonably timed? | *See above* |
| | Is the pace of the lesson effective? Not too fast, not too slow? | *Good pace in general, individual activities too long* |
| | How does the teacher differentiate activities? | *Not much differentiation – all pupils expected to produce more or less the same* |
| | How does the teacher address EAL/SEN pupil needs? | *Two EAL pupils would have benefited from simple written instructions, and extra oral instruction, plus additional guidance during activities* |
| | Is homework given, and is it part of the class homework timetable? What kinds of homework activity are given? | *No, shame!* |

**Figure 9.1**   (*Continued*)

| Year Group......... | Date/Time .............. | Teacher................... |
|---|---|---|
| **Focus** | **Observation Target** | **Comments** |
| | Was the plenary effective? | *Teacher brought the lesson to a close by asking pupils how far they'd got and what they thought they'd learnt – they're keen to respond to these questions, but don't seem aware of what they have or haven't learnt* |
| | Were the learning objectives/ outcomes achieved? Would you say 'real learning' is happening? Note the reasons for your response | *Not yet – need far more input, and understanding of written text in the TL before they can embark on writing themselves in terms of TL, slow progress I'd say at this stage – most of today's input will have to be repeated next lesson, similar to what happened today pupils generally motivated though, only when they become unclear or unable to manage the learning activity does motivation (and behaviour) start to dip* |
| **Assessment** | What opportunities for informal assessment are evident in the lesson? | *Whole-group oral work; moving around more in pair work would provide good opportunity* |
| | What assessment strategies does the teacher employ? | *No formal recording as yet; informal recording in post-lesson evaluation* |
| | Is there evidence of AfL? | *Pupils encouraged to reflect on how and what they are learning; some evidence that this is feeding into planning* |
| | Do pupils have insight into their own attainment and progress? | *Teacher is introducing individual 'record sheets' which he has discussed with pupils already – they appear very interested in this approach* |

**Figure 9.1**   *(Continued)*

### Post-observation reflective evaluation

- *Whole-group oral work seems to work best when it lasts about 15 minutes – any longer and pupils tend to become somewhat disordered.*
- *The writing activity lacked coherence – more detailed instructions, and exemplars of short written text could be given, and discussed as a whole group; most pupils appeared to struggle with the volume of writing required.*
- *Pupil motivation generally high – flagged somewhat when activities went on too long, as did behaviour.*
- *Optimal activity time seems to be about 15 minutes whole-group oral or discussion work; no longer than 10 mins. for writing, which needs to be structured with lots of guidance.*
- *Lesson was 45 mins – seems to be an optimal time if individual activities well paced – though once a week may be inadequate in the longer term – the recap showed that most pupils had not retained much from the week before.*
- *SoW not yet created so hard to situate the lesson as part of medium- or longer-term planning; the previous two lesson plans look much the same as this, so not convinced progression is fully or successfully embedded into planning.*
- *TL could be used more by both teacher and pupils – praise and instructions were often in English.*
- *Pupils would benefit from hearing unknown and unfamiliar language in a familiar context.*
- *Pupils may benefit from being encouraged to build up their own vocabulary bank – they have no form of reference for previously learnt language.*
- *Homework would work well with this class – the gap between lessons is so long, they have no way of even marginally embedding language.*

## Planning your first lessons

Before you start your placement, you should have an understanding of the content and structure of the school's languages programme, and how you might be expected to contribute to it. To plan effectively, you should aim to gather as much information on the languages programme, the pupils, and the school vision for languages as you can. Read through existing SoW and lesson plans where they are available, and map out the structures and content of the lessons you will be teaching. Lesson mapping is particularly important where there are no existing SoW or lesson plans. Remember to work closely with your mentor, the Languages Subject Leader and the class teacher, discussing your ideas with them.

## Features of best practice: current focus areas for evaluating primary languages teaching

The recent Ofsted report, *Primary Languages in Initial Teacher Training* (2008) identified five key focus areas for evaluating trainees' teaching which serve as a useful framework for best practice when planning for teaching and learning, as well as providing a guide for post-lesson evaluation, and targets for professional development:

Area 1: Professional Values and Practice

Area 2: Subject Knowledge

Area 3: Planning

Area 4: Assessment

Area 5: Teaching and Class Management.

When planning lessons, it is important to take on board these five areas (see Chapters 3 and 4).

---

## Activity

### Primary languages programmes: identifying best practice

Discuss as a group the features of the primary languages you observed during school experience. Summarize key points, identifying drivers for, and barriers to, successful inclusion of languages in the curriculum, and outlining what you consider to be the most effective model for primary languages, giving reasons for your conclusions.

---

## Conclusion

The end of school experience in your training year is just the beginning of your whole teaching career. It is important to make full use of your initial training by further developing and extending your competences, knowledge and skills. Planning should continue although your lesson plans might not be so lengthy and evaluation is a natural part of the planning cycle. As a newly qualified teacher, it is useful to continue to observe colleagues teach, in your own school and in other schools where there is effective practice; indeed, peer observation is an ongoing way to engage in mutual learning and support. There is always something new to learn and improving practice, keeping a sense of enquiry and sharing knowledge are a large part of what it means to be a professional in a learning community.

# 10 Learning abroad

## Teacher professional placements and school trips

---

This chapter discusses:

- how to facilitate professional learning within a structured and collaborative overseas placement framework
- the benefits of the teachers' professional placement and trips for pupils
- how to enhance the whole-school cultural dimension of language learning.

---

## Introduction

The most significant feature of a primary languages specialism is the current four-week period spent in a primary school overseas. It provides an invaluable opportunity for professional learning in an international community of practice. While many trainees, particularly languages graduates, will have already travelled extensively, the intensive period to be spent abroad as part of the training course needs careful preparation in order for it to bring maximum benefit in terms of upskilling in cultural awareness and linguistic competence. The overseas professional placement also provides trainees with an invaluable comparative perspective: identifying strengths in education systems and teaching strategies in other countries can meaningfully inform practice in English classrooms. Similarly, the contacts that trainees make during their time overseas can form lifelong professional and personal friendships, with 'ready-made' links with primary schools in the target country which can facilitate learning partnerships between schools and pupils. This chapter considers the value of school trips for pupils that trainees may well, at some point, organize as part of primary languages provision, and the value of the placement in developing critical cultural awareness. To be successful, the overseas professional placement should:

- address the learning needs of trainees from all countries, which may require careful negotiation and some compromise;
- operate in a framework of professional development linked to the standards for QTS or their equivalent (for example the French *Compétences Professionnelles des Maîtres*);

## Professional Values
### Development and progression tool

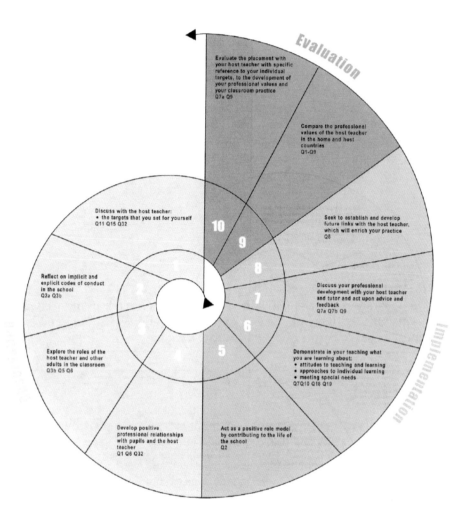

Evaluation

Evaluate the placement with your host teacher with specific reference to your individual targets, to the development of your professional values and your classroom practice
Q7a Q9

Compare the professional values of the host teacher in the home and host countries
Q1-Q9

Discuss with the host teacher:
• the targets that you set for yourself
Q11 Q15 Q32

Seek to establish and develop future links with the host teacher, which will enrich your practice
Q6

Reflect on implicit and explicit codes of conduct in the school
Q3a Q3b

Discuss your professional development with your host teacher and tutor and act upon advice and feedback
Q7a Q7b Q9

Explore the roles of the host teacher and other adults in the classroom
Q3h Q5 Q6

Demonstrate in your teaching what you are learning about:
• attitudes to teaching and learning
• approaches to individual learning
• meeting special needs
Q7Q10 Q18 Q19

Develop positive professional relationships with pupils and the host teacher
Q1 Q6 Q32

Act as a positive role model by contributing to the life of the school
Q2

Implementation

' 'Q + number' refers to English QTS standards

**Figure 10.1**    The assessment spirals: professional values and practice
*Source*: TDA (2007).

- have clearly defined learning objectives, which are understood by trainees, trainers and host schools;
- be realistic in terms of what a non-languages graduate may be reasonably expected to teach;
- be mapped out across the four weeks to ensure progression in professional learning.

The TDA has developed the *Common Reference Framework* in conjunction with the Ministries of Education in Belgium, Germany and France, and a Spanish framework is currently in development (see Figure 10.1: Professional Values). These frameworks provide a common ground for partners to work on, and one of the key features of the framework are the assessment 'spirals' which address four core competences:

1   Professional Values
2   Pedagogy and Practice
3   Linguistic Competence
4   Intercultural Understanding

They also make specific reference to the standards for QTS.

The application of the spirals in the assessment process embeds the overseas professional placement firmly into the PGCE programme, and allows tutors and trainees to set initial targets, track progress, and evaluate learning.

## Tutors talking

Here, a tutor talks about how she approached the establishment of overseas partnerships, and created a programme of professional learning:

> Our original partnerships were with Belgium and Germany, and we wanted to ensure that the four-week period overseas brought real benefits in terms of professional learning, as well as enhancing language skills and general intercultural competence. While a number of our Specialists are languages graduates, and have thus spend considerable time abroad as part of their studies, many of them as English language assistants in schools, a good number have A Level competence only, so we had to create a programme that addressed all their needs, and was realistic in terms of what we could expect from them. Everyone knows that building successful relationships takes time and understanding of each other's contexts, and we review the programmes every year. I drew up an information booklet for trainers and schools which were largely based on the CRF, and all key information, particularly the assessment templates, were provided in the target language. These are absolutely

crucial documents, something we can all refer to, and annotate as ideas strike us for how to improve things.

The booklet also forms the basis of our preparation session before the trainees go abroad – we set targets collaboratively and they discuss this with their mentors when they arrive in school.

Another key learning tool is the e-info exchange (see Box 10.1) which we set in motion as soon as possible. Socialization and establishing a community of practice are central to successful professional learning, and we felt that to keep the flow of communication smooth, and encourage people to participate, we should avoid making it a 'task' so each trainee writes in his or her own language – so while their writing skills in the target language may not be addressed, their reading skills definitely are. It also gives the trainees an idea of the professional language of teachers which in turn enriches their vocabulary. We start off with a general introduction, and a brief description of 'the school day', and progress to swapping information about particular aspects of the primary education, pedagogy, approaches to lesson planning, and so on. In this way, trainees have a wealth of background and insider information that really informs their practice overseas. We compare these approaches and strategies before and after the placement, embedding it into our understanding of how children develop and learn.

Trainees keep a reflective journal which informs their observations and reflections throughout the mentoring process. When we go over them, we can track progress really well with this, and summarize key learning points on the final assessment and self-assessment form. We then follow that up with whole-group feedback when the trainees return. As a group, they each choose a particular area of experience, and make a 10-minute presentation to the entire cohort followed by a Q&A session. In this way, they share their learning with those not on a specialist pathway, and this really helps them to focus on the exact nature of their learning.

All the various elements work together to provide a structured learning framework to which we can all refer, and within which we can all operate, really making the overseas placement an integral part of not just the specialism, but their training as primary practitioners in general.

## Box 10.1 An example of an e-info exchange:

**UK and German trainees sharing information about the structure and content of the primary school day, the languages programmes offered by the German school, and a description of the school's facilities and extra-curriculuar activities**

Hallo.

Ich wünsche euch erstmal natürlich auch ein gesundes, glückliches und erfolgreiches neues Jahr. Neben meinen Seminaren unterrichte ich 9 Stunden in der Woche und habe eine 5. Klasse in Englisch und eine 3. Klasse mit Deutsch und Sachunterricht (= Mischung aus social und life sciences). Die restlichen 3 Stunden hospitiere ich, bzw. helfe im Unterricht mit. Vorher habe ich an der Freien Universität und Humboldt Universität in Berlin studiert. Außerdem habe ich noch eine Ausbildung im Verlagsbereich gemacht und auch einige Jahre in diesem Bereich gearbeitet.

　　Meine Schule ist eine ganz normale Grundschule im Stadtteil＿dorf (Klassen 1–6). Die Schule ist im westlichen Zentrum der Stadt (der Ku damm ist ganz in der Nähe) und das Umfeld ist eher bürgerlich geprägt. Hier einige Daten zur Schule (Stand 8/2006):

- Anzahl Schüler: 530
- Anzahl Klassen: 21
- Anzahl Lehrer/Erzieher: 53
- Anteil ausländischer Schüler: ca. 19%
- Ausstattung: Computer (60 PCs, 30 Notebooks), große Aula, Musikraum, Naturwissenschaftsraum, Kunstraum, Theaterraum mit 90 Sitzplätzen, Sporthalle, Fußballfeld, Tennisfeld, Werkraum, Lehrküche, kl. Bibliothek . . .

Der Fremdsprachenunterricht beginnt in Berlin ab der 3. Klasse. Neben Englisch bietet unsere Schule auch Französisch als 1. Fremdsprache an. Hier die Anzahl der Unterrichtsstunden pro Woche à 45 Minuten:

- Klasse 3: 2 Stunden pro Woche
- Klasse 4: 3
- Klasse 5: 4
- Klasse 6: 5

Unsere Unterrichtszeiten:

　　1. Stunde　08.00–08.45
　　2. Stunde　08.50–09.35
　　*1. große Pause *
　　3. Stunde　09.55–10.40
　　4. Stunde　10.45–11.30

*2. große Pause *
5. Stunde          11.50–12.35
6. Stunde          12.40–13.25
*Mittagspause    13.30–14.15*
7. Stunde          14.15–15.00
8. Stunde          15.00–15.45

In den großen Pausen sind die Schüler auf dem Pausenhof (bei Regen bleiben die Schüler drinnen). Die Lehrer machen Aufsichten, sind im Lehrerzimmer oder in ihren Klassen.

Wir sind eine verlässliche Halbtagsgrundschle (kostenlos). Das bedeutet, die Schüler sind in der Zeit von 7.30–13.30 Uhr betreut. Daneben gibt es noch eine kostenpflichtige Ganztagsbetreuung (Hort) mit folgenden Betreuungszeiten:

- Frühbetreuung: 06:00–07:30 Uhr
- Nachmittagsbetreuung: 13:30–16:00 Uhr
- Spätbetreuung: 16:00–18:00 Uhr

Dann gibt es bei uns auch noch den Hebel-Club (= Schülerclub), ein offenes Freizeitangebot an die Schüler in der Zeit von 12–16.00 Uhr. Die Schüler werden von einer Erzieherin betreut. Die Nutzung ist kostenlos, Spenden sind jedoch erwünscht. Organisiert wird das Ganze von den Eltern.

Außerdem gibt es bei uns eine Mensa:

*Essensausgabe von 11:30–14 Uhr*

Preis für ein Essen incl. Getränk z. Zt. 1,85€

Anbei schicke ich euch einen Stundenentwurf vom November zu. Die Stunde lief ganz gut, war aber etwas zu einfach für meine 5. Klasse, das heißt der Lernzuwachs war nicht angemessen.

Ich freue mich schon darauf, euch alle endlich in einigen Tagen kennen zu lernen. Liebe Grüße aus einem winterlichen Berlin,
Denise

# The reflective journal

As discussed, the reflective journal is a key professional learning tool. During the overseas placement, you should keep a reflective journal focusing on your experiences of teaching and learning in your target country, your improving language skills, and deepening awareness of the cultural, social and demographic profile of that country.

Here, Simon reflects on the teaching strategies he has observed in a Year 2 Mathematics class, and evaluates the impact of those strategies on pupil learning. Crucially, while he acknowledges the strengths of what he has seen, he questions to what extent some pupils are best served by those strategies, and evaluates the benefits of independent learning:

## Trainees reflecting

It is undoubtedly the promotion of independent learning for every child which is the main approach to teaching in this particular primary school. This independent learning style becomes apparent in Year 2 right from the very first lesson of the week. Designated as 'free choice of work', children have the opportunity to choose a maths or literacy activity which they then complete themselves. These activities take many forms; cards which are simply covered in acetate and filled in with removable wipe pen; boards which use coloured sliding buttons to allow matching of question and answer; cards with indentations down either side which allow matching of question and answer using elastic bands; simple games such as dice combinations and logic puzzles. Admittedly children are restricted in the activities that they can do depending on their current level. Naturally a child cannot be expected to complete an activity involving subtraction if they are still struggling with addition. Therefore activities are split into different blocks, e.g. addition, subtraction, etc. with five activities in each block. Only when one block is complete can a child move on to the next block. The key, however, is that children still choose their own activity and complete it independently without any teacher input. Furthermore, they check their answers against those which are given on the reverse of each card and when completed cross off the activity on a chart at the front of the classroom – further promoters of independent learning.

Independent learning is further encouraged in mathematics. In a week comprising of five 45-minute maths lessons, not once do I see the class teacher teach a maths concept to the class as a whole. Nor do I see a plenary with lessons regularly concluding with children finishing the sum or sentence they are on. Children simply work independently from two textbooks which are specifically designed to fit the maths curriculum. Children work through the pages specified for completion in a list on the blackboard. This means that one pupil is on page 15, adding one-digit numbers to two-digit numbers whereas another pupil is on page 30, subtracting two-digit multiples of ten from two-digit numbers. In other words children work at their own pace to their own level. Should a child manage to complete a whole page without help from either teacher or peers they acquire 'Expert' status and are given the opportunity to explain the relevant mathematical concept to a struggling child. The expert makes other pupils aware of his status by writing on a Post-it note at the relevant page of a textbook left open to the whole class. A struggling child then turns to the page of difficulty in this textbook and seeks help from the expert – another example of the child's independence towards learning. By teaching the concept, the expert also firmly secures the understanding of the concept in their own mind.

The same independent learning policy also applies in literacy with children randomly choosing activity cards designed to cover the literacy curriculum which cover different rules of spelling . . . and then proceed to test literal comprehension and sentence writing. On reflection, I believe that independent learning through continuous textbook work is a successful teaching method however it cannot stand alone. Children must also be given the chance to learn actively in maths and literacy through other methods which are covered effectively in this particular class through the ready availability of widespread resources for varied and engaging learning and experimentation. I believe the exclusive use of textbooks creates two main problems. Firstly, and most obviously, a lack of variety and ultimately boredom and disengagement with the subject. Secondly, when children are allowed to work at their own pace and to their own level, are the children who are further behind really lower-ability pupils or are they simply not putting in the required effort? It strikes me in this particular Year 2 class that several children fall into the latter category.

## Trainees talking

Trainees were asked a series of questions about their time overseas with regard to their learning:

Q: *How would you characterize your key learning during your time in primary schools overseas?*

### English trainee in Belgium

A: I feel the most valuable experience was learning about schools from another culture generally. It was really helpful to see what things I felt could be improved over there and the types of things which could improve practice in England. For me, personally, I really liked the school atmosphere in that it was more laid back over there and I felt that pupils were treated more equally to teachers. The teachers seemed to interact with pupils on more of an equal basis. This gave the impression that there were higher expectations of pupils, i.e. as pupils were spoken to less like 'children'.

### English trainee in Germany

A: I feel my professional development was enhanced by spending time in a combination of English and overseas schools during my PGCE year. The variety of experiences this afforded was valuable, in addition to the opportunities for comparison between the systems. This was especially pertinent to my ideas about MFL teaching in the English Primary sector.

Q: *To what extent was the time spent in England/overseas useful for your understanding of different cultural contexts?*

### English trainee in Germany

A: I found my time in Germany very useful in understanding the diversity of different cultural contexts. However, following my final placement in Manchester, the similarities between culturally diverse areas of England and Germany have become more apparent than the cultural differences between the two countries.

### Belgian trainee in England

A: Il y a pleins de différences culturelles entre l'Angleterre et la Belgique, ce voyage m'a permis encore une fois de me rendre compte des richesses culturelles de chaque pays mais surtout de la richesse d'en découvrir un maximum pour mieux comprendre chaque nouveau pays.

Q: *To what extent does your understanding of the primary education system in England/ overseas help you in teaching English/German/French/Spanish in your own country?*

### English trainee in Belgium

A: There's more old-fashioned teaching of language over there – pupils seemed bored sometimes, less variation in activities, not very fun or motivating, lack of ICT and interesting resources. It gave me more inspiration and showed the importance of making language teaching fun and engaging and appealing. However, some aspects are better than in England, grammar focus for example really helps pupils in their home language and also helps them greatly for learning additional language.

### English trainee in Germany

A: I found the focus on grammar in German lessons a refreshing change and I have tried to bring more of this into my own literacy lessons in England. Also, the lack of ICT in German classrooms has brought the use of such elements in my own classroom into perspective and has helped me to see that ICT does not necessarily equal success.

Q: *How might you use the knowledge you gained in your professional activity overseas as teachers in your own country?*

### English trainee in Germany

A: While I came to the conclusion that the amount of time, and therefore importance allocated to language teaching was the clinching factor in assuring the relative success of the German system, there were also several aspects of the experience that I will use in my own professional activity. The use of song and games was especially successful in the German classes I worked in, even at an upper junior level. This approach already forms the majority of my language teaching practice, and is proving highly successful in my Year 2 class.

### Belgian trainee in England

A: En Angleterre, j'ai appris à préparer mes leçons de façon très précises parce que j'étais peu sûre de moi à cause de mon niveau en anglais. Alors je prévoyais même les imprévus et ça m'a permis de prendre de l'assurance en classe.

Q: *Have you kept in touch with your English/overseas primary school, or do you plan to use the contacts in England/overseas to set up any kind of link between the children you teach, and the children at your overseas schools?*

### English trainee in Germany

A: I have kept in touch and plan to set up links once I take up the role of MFL coordinator in the next academic year. I look forward to setting up postal and email links between the schools.

Q: *Was the information exchange via email prior to coming to England useful?*

### Belgian trainee in England

A: Les échanges ont été très utiles pour se rassurer, se préparer, imaginer un peu les différences avant de les découvrir en life!!

Q: *Do you have any other comments?*

### English trainee in Belgium

A: Great experience, culturally and to see difference between language and other subject teaching there and in England. Can use their strategies and see what English schools are more positive at/need to improve upon – pass on info to various schools and also apply to my professional development.

## Activity

After your overseas professional placement, in small groups discuss and define your key learning. Consider also to what extent this learning may be replicated in a home-based programme, and feed back to the whole group.

## Real-world learning: enhancing pupil experience in authentic contexts

The trainees have derived much benefit from their overseas experience and have learnt to compare critically different systems and ways of doing things. They have experienced culture as a living, dynamic process, reflecting Street's view of culture 'as a verb' (1993: 2), there finding points of concurrence as well as of contestation, disconfirming as well as confirming expectations. The students have engaged with issues in an ethnographic experience in a participant observer role, and have, as Roberts writes 'involve[d] themselves in the lives of others and yet are able to stand back and reflect on those lives' (1997: 64), Ultimately, you will want to provide the children with such rich and transformational learning.

As we discussed in Chapter 4, a language and the cultures of the people who speak it are interlinked and an effective primary languages programme will have a rich cultural frame. There is a plethora of resources to use that includes 'virtual culture' of all kinds on the internet as well as books, artefacts and visuals. This brings culture into the classroom and allows the children to develop their cultural awareness in the familiarity of their usual learning environment. In the secure environment of the classroom, the learners can then go beyond the anecdotal, the touristy folklore and the stereotyping and begin to develop an intercultural competence in a more systematic and critical way. Language teachers need to go beyond the confines of their classroom and seek to enhance the whole school cultural awareness. This can be done in simple ways by, for example, ensuring display material in the target languages, posters, contributions in assembly and at special events such as ensuring a supply of foreign language materials in book weeks. There are school exchanges of materials to organize, visitors to welcome from other countries and the cultural and linguistic diversity of the children themselves to be celebrated. The deepening of cultural awareness in the class and the interculturality of each child can thus be developed not only in the languages classroom but in the whole-school learning community as part of its cultural learning agenda.

The first trip abroad (and 'abroad' may well have been the Isle of Wight or similar for some readers) must feature for most of us as one of the most memorable experiences in our lives. Much of the excitement was lived in the build up and the anticipation of the event and at the *point de départ*, perhaps more so than at the *point d'arrivée*. At this point it was probable that an element of culture shock perhaps overwhelmed us momentarily until successful adaptation in this initial intercultural encounter. This is how one languages teacher recalls her first experience abroad: 'In spite of everything I had learnt at school, it was still so foreign and exotic in some ways and I was astonished that I had to use my German so it was a good job I knew some basic German for directions and things like that.' This is a common reaction when experiencing something new and the emotions of engaging with 'foreignness' should not be underestimated, especially where our young learners are concerned. One Head emphasized that: 'One reason why our annual week away with Yr 6 is successful is because we spend the whole year working on it.'

Most language teachers, with fond memories of their own visits abroad, see a school trip as an essential part of the languages provision and work towards this as one of the key objectives in the language learning programme. Furthermore, cultural learning and intercultural competence are key strands underpinning the language learning enterprise. It is traditionally a key feature of KS3/4 languages programmes, and we would argue that there are immeasurable benefits from providing the same real-world language experience for children at KS2. The trip, be it to France or anywhere else, is often scheduled towards the end of Year 6 as the culmination to the KS2 stage of learning, although in some cases, it takes place at the end of Year 5 so that ongoing references can be made during Year 6 and learning grounded in the experience. A great many schools have a link with an activity centre or are involved in school exchanges or town-twinning arrangements. The benefit of these is the assured cooperation of the other side and the rapport and continuity that can be developed over repeated visits.

---

## Teachers talking

One teacher explains in an interview why this kind of visit is the most suitable for young pupils, followed by the views of a group of pupils of the trip.

Q: *What kind of trip do you organize and why?*

A: We organize a 3-day trip to a purpose-designed centre that the LA recommends in Northern France. It is an activity centre so there are lots of things for the children to do. It is much better than going to a hotel as the children can be together as a community and it is easier for the teachers to monitor the children.

Q: *What are the benefits for the pupils?*

A: Above all, it provides an opportunity for bonding. The children play with children they would not normally play with and discover other children's interests they did not know about. It gives the children a sense of independence with many children away from home for the first time. They have to make their own beds, for example, although some children just stand there waiting for someone else to make their beds so it's good learning for them. They are not allowed to take mobiles so that they are not ringing home all the time nor being rung. It also gives them an insight into the culture without immersing them in it so they always feel secure.

Q: *Do the children improve their language skills?*

A: It's more that they get the chance to practise what they have been learning and see that it works. There are set things that they have to do such as asking for water at meals, buying an ice cream, asking for a stamp to send a postcard home. Some of them use their initiative and use more French, mainly the confident children. It's a confidence thing and it's different using French in France when you are speaking to be understood as opposed to using it in the classroom.

Q: *Are there any problems that arise when you are away?*

A: Very few. Occasionally children fall out and we have to deal with that. Sometimes a child cannot sleep at night and we have to sit with them. There's no time for them to get homesick as we keep them busy as we know they are quite vulnerable. On arrival, they write a postcard immediately, more as a comfort thing, and we get them into routines.

Q: *Are there any benefits for the teachers?*

A: It is no holiday for the teachers! But it is nice to see the children outside of the classroom and how they develop different friendships. Also we can practise our French, get our wine and chocolates.

Q: *What about organizational issues and risk management?*

A: We work on preparing the trip all year, collecting money and organizing trips as we do lots of excursions and these have to be booked. It can be difficult to get confirmation, especially on the telephone if staff don't speak French and that's where a French-speaking parent has been really helpful. Risk management means you have to have visited the place before you take children and evaluate the risks and rules that you will need. The centre, for example, is in magnificent grounds and there is a forest so the children are not allowed out on their own other than on the patio at the front of the building.

Q: *Are the children Ok with the food? On my first school trip, the first meal the children were faced with a mountain of 'lentilles-saucisse' which they found a bit intimidating!*

A: Well, the cooks are French but they are used to preparing food that the children will enjoy. They have a 4-course meal every night and that is part of the cultural learning. We ask the children always to try something of each course so they always get enough to eat and usually enjoy most of it. We take some provisions such as biscuits so that there is always something and the children have a drink and a biscuit in the evening.

Q: *What follow-up work do you do after the trip?*

A: The first thing they do is a presentation to the rest of the school and parents in an assembly. The children did their own assembly with a PowerPoint, charting the whole journey. They will do more on this in the leavers' final assembly with the funny bits. We also have photos up on the walls and examples of the corn dollies they made at the farm we went to.

Q: *What is the most valuable thing about this trip?*

A: It's a really valuable KS2 experience not just from the French point of view and it's about growing up.

## Pupils talking

Pupils talking in a group interview about the same trip:

Q: *Did you enjoy your recent trip to France?*

A: YES!!!

Q: *What did you like in particular?*

A: We liked the rides at the Bagatelle (theme park), the football and table tennis, the trip to Nausicaa (oceanarium), the trip to the farm, the dorms, the outside of where we stayed which was quite posh, the woods, the food..!

Q: *What French did you use in these things?*

A: We had to ask for water and a cloth in French, and other things at breakfast. We had to greet people in shops and on trips in French and ask how much things were if you had to pay for a ride.

Q: *What did you learn about France?*

A: We learnt to be very polite to people we didn't know and to behave and no jumping around. Their animals are very similar to ours and the people are mainly friendly and if you don't understand they will speak in English.

Q: *Was there anything you found difficult or didn't like?*

A: The queues for the rides were annoying and sometimes you couldn't understand what they were saying or you did but didn't know how to reply. It took time to get used to the food, the chicken was too salty and the cheese was really ripe. There weren't any frogs' legs.

Q: *Would you like to go to France again?*

A: YES!! But we do need to learn some normal French and not just animals and colours.

Q: *What advice would you give to next year's children going on the trip?*

A: Child A: Learn a bit more French so you can use more phases.
Child B: Just enjoy it.
Child C: Tell your mum not to be nervous.

When comparing the perspectives, several mirror images can be found in the responses. The teachers, for example, emphasize the importance of the children's play, activity and adventure and these are what the children immediately identify as key factors of enjoyment. The children also confirm that their use of language is limited but that it is naturally occurring in authentic contexts and that usually what they have been practising in class works but when it doesn't, they can resort to another strategy. The children appear to have remarkable coping strategies and take the challenges in their stride. This concurs with the teacher that the trip serves as a powerful learning opportunity for social and interpersonal skills. Furthermore, Barrett's review of research indicates that 'children sometimes exhibit more positive affect towards countries they have visited' (2007: 71). Worthy of investigation is the point raised by the children themselves that a different type of language, and we may confidently assume transactional language, would have been very useful. In the light of a language-need audit of a school trip, it is useful to think about what language could be pre-taught and rehearsed by way of extended utterance in addition to and going beyond simple greetings and very basic requests. These children indicated the following as a starter:

- I am sorry, I don't understand.
- Can you speak English please?
- What's his name? e.g. of farm animal
- Just a little.
- Thank you but I don't like it.
- Can I have some more?
- That's nice, I like that.
- We've won/lost.
- Can we ... ?

The teacher agreed that this kind of follow-up would be useful as a way to extend the children's linguistic knowledge and beneficial for the next year's children. There is a clear indication that the children need more at sentence level rather than word level, more connectives, more question formats and to be able to manipulate the language. The children would then be able to ask about a horse's name at the farm and see how this structure relates to saying their own name or asking someone else their name.

## Building on learning: after the trip abroad

As the teacher pointed out earlier in the chapter, much of the work that contributed to the success of their trip took place before and after the actual journey. Preparation had included looking at photos and videos of previous visits, examining documentation about the accommodation and brochures concerning the excursions. The children had also practised little role-plays, e.g. asking for water with their meals, please and thank you, how much, and so on. After the event, the children had discussed the trip and had prepared presentations using their IT and presentational skills and made posters for a whole-school display. Cultural learning should not just surround the trip but needs to be part of the ongoing language learning provision. Videoconferencing is an ideal way to keep in touch with contacts that are made and bring real culture into the school.

## Conclusion

Spending time in another country, for both trainee teachers and pupils, are profitable and enjoyable in different ways for every individual. We each engage in our own way and develop our own cultural awareness and intercultural competence. Not everything is to our liking and sometimes we are challenged in our thinking and in our feelings. For trainees, the overseas professional development can make key contributions to overall professional development, and, for children, it provides a real-world experience of a language and culture. Children make it clear what they like and do not like but in an open and non-prejudiced way. Unfortunately, some experiences abroad serve to reinforce stereotypes and create anxiety and these are situations where the learning of tolerance and understanding are crucial. Yet through these varied experiences can come powerful transformational learning that opens our eyes to new ways of knowing and being that change our outlook on the world forever. We become empowered and develop an critical cultural awareness that corresponds to the skill and ability to *savoir s'engager*. The humble beginnings of primary language learning in the classroom set seed for wonderful opportunities and life options and the chance to become an active cosmopolitan citizen in later life. This is truly an astonishing legacy of the task and mission awaiting the primary languages teacher.

# Epilogue

## The primary languages teacher as researcher

### Learning from the 'inside-out'

This chapter concludes this book but, at the same time, it opens the way to the next stage in developing your role as a critically reflective practitioner through continuing professional development, enquiry and research. Some teachers mistakenly assume that educational research is something to do with academics and higher level study and operates at a level of abstraction that is far removed from the classroom. This is to misunderstand what research is and can be, and the potential value and usefulness for classroom teachers. Indeed, you as trainee teacher will spend a great deal of time observing, evaluating and reflecting on practice and are thus a natural researcher. As Brighouse and Woods comment: 'Teachers are natural researchers, in the sense that all teaching is based on inquiry and the response of the pupils provide ready evidence as to the effectiveness of various teaching and learning approaches' (1999: 42).

You as a teacher are uniquely positioned to research your own practice 'inside-out', i.e. starting from what goes on in your own classroom, and that of colleagues, that will include the successes, the discrepancies and the unexpected. Research and theorizing are, as Cochran-Smith and Lytle write: 'an important part of the teachers' learning experience and crucially, an opportunity to play a role in generating a knowledge base 'inside-out' emanating from neither theory nor practice alone but from critical reflection on the intersection of the two' (1993: 15).

### Research experiences

You will have had many opportunities to reflect on such 'intersections', for example, in group work with your peers and in personal reflections. You will have used, as part of your ongoing systematic enquiry in your training, many research tools such as questionnaires, interviews, observation and documentary analysis routinely as part of your explorations into learning, teaching and assessment, thus developing an awareness of both qualitative and quantitative research methods. As a result of this research, you will have obtained a large amount of data that will have given you insights into the ways children learn, the effectiveness of teaching approaches and all the activities in the primary languages classroom. It is important to continue to nurture your sense of enquiry and to remain observant and alert to being able to respond to that most fundamental research question of 'what is going on?' and to consider ways of how practice might be improved. Indeed, school improvement is not something that happens as a result of top-down decisions but it happens in the classroom on the basis of the many modest decisions and actions taken by teachers.

## Topics for research

Regarding the topics raised in this book, there are many issues that need a personal response from you in supporting you to develop your professional persona and that create possibilities for worthwhile research. As a starting point for your reflections on the current research agenda in primary languages, we would suggest the following:

### School improvement and managing change

- How does the inclusion of modern languages in the primary curriculum contribute to overall school improvement, and how are teachers adapting their professional identity to meet the challenge?
- What are the key drivers for, and barriers to, successful implementation of new educational initiatives?
- Do current curricular models for the provision of primary languages achieve discernible benefits in learning across the curriculum?

### The primary languages practitioner

- How are we preparing our teachers for primary languages, and what constitutes good practice in initial teacher education and programmes of professional development?
- A key point about planning is that it should be an aid to progressing pupil learning. Given that progression is a crucial factor in a pupil's cross-phase language learning trajectory, how can we define progression in conceptual terms and how does planning support this process?

### Understanding acquisition of a second language in a classroom environment

- How do children acquire a second language in classrooms? What processes are involved, and to what extent does current practice ensure competence in the target language? Is our definition of 'competence' in the context of primary languages reasonable and achievable?
- Does younger really equal better? How do we measure whether an early start can lead to an increase in linguistic competence?
- Consider the differences and similarities and think about how classroom contextual factors and other variables might impact on the success or otherwise of classroom learning.

## Effective practice in early language teaching

- What strategies are successful in the primary languages classroom?
- How can an understanding of child language development contribute to meaningful teaching and successful learning in the primary languages classroom?

## Assessment

- Which theories of learning underpin an Assessment for Learning approach and how can these inform effective planning and language teaching?
- How can the consistent use of self- and peer assessment in the languages classroom lead to greater learner autonomy?

## Subject leadership

- What are the key features of effective subject leadership? How does leadership mesh with the managerial aspects of the subject leader role such as accountability?
- How does effective subject leadership contribute to effective teaching and learning?

## Transition

- On the basis of research on transition, and from the perspective of learning theories and observations of pupil learning, what are the learning needs and the potential for learning of pupils at KS2 and how can these be exploited in the primary languages classroom to enable productive learning at KS3?
- 'Language learning at KS2 leading to a "renaissance" in language learning at KS3 and beyond.' What factors support or refute this view?

## Learning in international contexts

- How can pupils engage with the 'savoirs' as defined, for example, by Byram (2008, for example), in their primary language learning before, during and after a visit/trip of some kind?
- Do you agree that in taking an ethnographic stance while spending time abroad, primary language teachers can develop intercultural competence?

# The teacher-researcher as agent of change

You will doubtless have questions of your own and issues you want to pursue. It is important that you follow your interest as Loughram urges, 'seeking answers to questions . . . which are important in the teaching and learning environment' (1999: 3). In such a way, your learning will be sustained and you will enact that agency that is a very special feature of the teaching profession, and that will enable you to be a creative and innovative primary languages teacher and a critically reflective practitioner.

To conclude, there are enormous benefits to individual teachers in exploring, researching and improving their practice as part of professional development and growth: this is the essence of lifelong learning. At a very pragmatic level, this approach is a prerequisite to the expectation that all new entrants to the profession will acquire Masters level qualification. Most important of all, just as our young learners experience the excitement and challenge of learning a new language and new ways of thinking and seeing their world through this powerful experience, so does the language teacher mirror that process and that experience.

# Appendix

## Key websites

### Primary modern languages

www.primarylanguages.org.uk
   With ideas for lessons, teaching activities, information on integrating languages across the curriculum, and video-clips

http://www.qca.org.uk/qca_11752.aspx
   The new QCA Schemes of Work for French, German and Spanish – 24 units designed for learning across KS2

http://www.standards.dfes.gov.uk/primary/publications/languages/framework/
   The KS2 Framework for Languages in full

www.nacell.org.uk
   The National Advisory Centre for Early Language Learning – with a particular focus on early language learning

### General modern languages

www.cilt.org.uk
   The National Centre for Languages, with links to other relevant sites, ideas for teaching and general information. Also includes links to extremely useful email discussion groups

www.all.org.uk
   The Association for Language Learning – the subject association for language professionals, with information about their key publications, including *Language Learning Journal*

### Primary curriculum

http://www.standards.dfes.gov.uk/primaryframeworks/
   Primary Frameworks – links to PDFs and other relevant information

http://www.standards.dfes.gov.uk/primaryframeworks/literacy/learningobjectives/Strands/
   The learning objectives for each individual literacy strand

http://www.standards.dfes.gov.uk/primaryframeworks/downloads/PDF/PF_Literacy_by_year_alt.pdf

The literacy strands by year group, very useful to use in planning for progression

http://www.standards.dfes.gov.uk/primaryframeworks/literacy/ictapplications/
For ideas on how to integrate ICT activities into your language programme, refer
to the ICT strand of the primary framework

## Web-based information and resources

www.assetlanguages.org.uk – The Languages Ladder

http://curriculum.qca.org.uk/ – the National Curriculum site

http://www.britishcouncil.org/learning-world – particularly the partnerships and 'spotlight on' section

www.globalgateway.org – a wealth of information and links with a focus on the international dimension

www.etwinning.net; www.epals.net – useful information for teachers seeking to link with overseas schools

http://www.teachers.tv/ – useful video clips and ideas for teaching – simply search under 'primary' then 'modern foreign languages'

http://www.teachernet.gov.uk/teachingandlearning/ – a valuable information and resource bank for teachers across all key stages

http://www.ttrb.ac.uk/ – the Teacher Training Resource Bank

www.bbc.co.uk/schools/primaryfrench; www.bbc.co.uk/schools/primarygerman; www.bbc.co.uk/primaryspanish – BBC primary languages sites

http://www.ltscotland.org.uk/mfle/ – the Learning and Teaching Scotland site for modern languages

http://www.primaryresources.co.uk/mfl/mfl.htm – a resource bank created by teachers

http://wsgfl.westsussex.gov.uk/ccm/navigation/curriculum/modern-foreign-languages/key-stage-2/

http://www.ngfl-cymru.org.uk/eng/vtc-home/vtc-ks2-home/vtc-ks2-french
the West Sussex Grid for Learning site and the National Grid for Learning Cymru both provide a wealth of ideas and resources for primary languages

http://www.coe.int/
the Council of Europe website has information and links to a range of resources and information, including the European Languages Portfolio

# Bibliography

Alexander, R. (2008) The primary review: emerging perspectives on childhood. Keynote lecture presented at the GTC conference on Childhood, Wellbeing and Primary Education, London.

ALL (Association for Language Learning) (1997) *Draft Policy on Primary Modern Languages*. Rugby: ALL.

Barrett, M. (2007) *Children's Knowledge: Beliefs and Feelings about Nations and National Groups*. London: Psychology Press.

Beaton, R. (1990) The many sorts of error, in B. Page (ed.) *What Do You Mean it's Wrong?* London: CILT.

Bennett, S. N. (1975) Weighing the evidence: A review of 'Primary French in the Balance', *British Journal of Educational Psychology*, 45: 337–40.

Black, P., Harrison, C., Lee, C., Marshall, B. and Wiliam, D. (2003) *Assessment for Learning: Putting it into Practice*. Maidenhead: Open University Press.

Black, P. and Wiliam, D. (1998) *Inside the Black Box: Raising Standards through Classroom Assessment*. London: King's College London.

Bolster, A., Balandier-Brown, C. and Rea-Dickins, P. (2004) Young learners of modern foreign languages and their transition to the secondary phase: a lost opportunity? *Language Learning Journal*, 30: 35–41.

Brighouse, T. and Woods, P. (1999) *How to Improve Your School*. London: Methuen.

Burrows, D. (2004) *Tidying the Cupboard?* Nottingham: National College for School Leadership.

Burstall, C., Jamieson, M., Cohen, S. and Hargreaves, M. (1974) *Primary French in the Balance*. Slough: NFER.

Byram, M. (1997) *Teaching and Assessing Intercultural Competence*. Clevedon: Multilingual Matters.

Byram, M. (2008) *From Foreign Language Education to Education for Intercultural Citizenship: Essays and Reflections*. Clevedon: Multilingual Matters.

Cable, C. et al. (2008) *Language Learning at Key Stage 2: A Longitudinal Study – Interim Finding from the First Year*. Research Brief DCSF-RBX-08-08.

Cameron, L. (2001) *Teaching Languages to Young Learners*. Cambridge: Cambridge University Press.

Clarke, S. (2001) *Unlocking Formative Assessment. Practical Strategies for Enhancing Pupils' Learning in the Primary School*. London: Hodder and Stoughton.

Clarke, S. (2003) *Enriching Feedback in the Primary Classroom*. London: Hodder and Stoughton.

Cochran-Smith, M. and Lytle, S. (1993) *Inside Outside: Teacher Research and Knowledge*. New York: Teachers College Press.

Council of Europe (2001) *Common European Framework of Reference for Languages: Learning, Teaching, Assessment*. Cambridge: Cambridge University Press.

Curtain, H. and Pesola, C. A. (1994) *Languages and Children: Making the Match*. New York: Longman.

Dart, B., Boulton-Lewis, G., Brownlee, J. and McCrindle, A. (1998) Change in knowledge of learning and teaching through journal writing, *Research Papers in Education*, 13(3): 291–318.

DCSF (2008) *The Independent Review of the Primary Curriculum*, PPAPG/D35(3931)/1208/ 13, available for download from http://publications.teachernet.gov.uk

Dearing, R. and King, L. (2007) *Languages Review*. Nottingham: DfES Publications.

Dewey, J (1933) *How We Think: A Restatement of the Relation of Reflective Teaching to the Education Process*. Chicago: Henry Regnery.

Dewey, J. (1966) *Democracy and Education: An Introduction to the Philosophy of Education*. New York: Free Press.

DfE (1993) *The Initial Training of Primary School Teachers: New Criteria for Courses*, 14/93. London: DfE.

DfES (2002a) *National Curriculum: Handbook for Primary Teachers in England*. Nottingham: DfES Publications.

DfES (2002b) National Languages Strategy, *Languages for All: Languages for Life*. Nottingham: DfES Publications.

DfES (2003) *Excellence and Enjoyment: A Strategy for Primary Schools*. Nottingham: DfES.

DfES (2004a) *Every Child Matters: Change for Children*. Nottingham: DfES Publications.

DfES (2004b) *Five Year Strategy for Children and Learners*. Nottingham: DfES Publications.

DfES (2004c) *Excellence and Enjoyment: Learning and Teaching in the Primary Years – Designing Opportunities for Learning*. Nottingham: DfES Publications.

DfES (2005) *Key Stage 2 Framework for Languages, Parts 1 and 2*. Nottingham: DfES Publications.

Doyé, P. (1999) *The Intercultural Dimension: Foreign Language Education in the Primary School*. Berlin: Cornelsen.

Driscoll, P. and Frost, D. (eds) (1999) *The Teaching of Modern Foreign Languages in the Primary School*. London: Routledge.

Driscoll, P., Jones, J. and Macrory, G. (2004) *The Provision of Foreign Language Learning for Pupils at Key Stage 2*, DfES Research Report 572. Nottingham: DfES Publications.

Driscoll, P., Jones, J., Martin, C., Graham-Matheson, L., Dismore, H. and Sykes, R. (2004) A systematic review of the characteristics of effective foreign language teaching to pupils between the ages of 7 and 11, in *Research Evidence in Education Library*. London: EPPI-Centre, Social Science Research Unit, Institute of Education.

Earley, P. and Weindling, D. (2004) *Understanding School Leadership*. London: Paul Chapman Publishing.

Galton, M., Gray, J. and Rudduck, J. (1999) *The Impact of School Transitions and Transfers on Pupil Progress and Attainment*. Research Report 131. London: DfES.

Hall, K. and Hardin, A. (2003) A systematic review of effective literacy teaching in the 4 to 14 range of mainstream school. In: *Research Evidence in Education Library*, London: EPPI-Centre, Social Science Research Unit, Institute of Education.

Harris, A., Day, C., Hopkins, D., Hadfield, M., Hargreaves, A. and Chapman, C. (2003) *Effective Leadership for School Improvement*. London: RoutledgeFalmer.

Hawkins, E. (1981) *Modern Languages in the Curriculum*. Cambridge: Cambridge Educational.

Hawkins, E. (1996) *30 Years of Language Teaching*. London: CILT.

Heath, H. (1998) Keeping a reflective practice diary: a practical guide. *Nurse Education Today*, 18: 592–8.

Holly, M. (1989) Reflective writing and the spirit of inquiry, *Cambridge Journal of Education*, 19(1): 71–80.

Hopkins, D. and Jackson, D. (2003) Building the capacity for leading and learning, in A. Harrison et al. (eds) *Effective Leadership for School Improvement*. London: RoutledgeFalmer.

Hopkins, D., Ainscow, M. and West, M. (1994) *School Improvement in an Era of Change*. London: Cassell.

Hoy, P. (1976) *The Conditions for Success*. Strasbourg: Council of Europe.

Hoy, P. (1977) *The Early Teaching of Modern Languages*. London: The Nuffield Foundation.

Jones, J. (2005) Foreign languages in the primary school in England: a new pupil learning continuum, *Francophonie*, Spring (31): 3–7.

Jones, J. (2010) The role of Assessment for Learning in the management of primary to secondary transition: implications for language teachers, *Language Learning Journal*, in press.

Jones, J. and Coffey, S. (2006) *Modern Foreign Languages 5–11: A guide for Teachers*. London: Routledge.

Jones, J. and Wiliam, D. (2008) *Modern Foreign Languages Inside the Black Box*. London: GLA Assessment.

Kirsch, C. (2008) *Teaching Foreign Languages in the Primary School*. London: Continuum.

Kramsch, C. (1993) *Context and Culture in Language Teaching*. Oxford: Oxford University Press.

Lazaro, C. M. (1963) *Report on Foreign Language Teaching in British Primary Schools*. Nuffield Foreign Languages Teaching Materials Project, Occasional Paper No. 1, Leeds.

Lightbown, P. and Spada, N. (1999) *How Languages are Learned*, 2nd edn. Oxford: Oxford University Press.

Loughram, J. (ed.) (1999) *Researching Teaching: Methodologies and Practices for Understanding Pedagogy*. London: Falmer Press.

Macrory, G. (2008) Modern Foreign Languages (MFL): Beyond The Curriculum, in R. Boys and E. Spink (eds) *Teaching the Foundation Subjects*. London: Continuum.

Macrory, G. and McLachlan, A. (2009) Bringing modern languages into the primary curriculum in England: investigating effective practice in teacher education, *European Journal of Teacher Education*, 32(3): 261–72.

Martin, C. (2000) *An Analysis of National and International Research on the Provision of Modern Languages in Primary Schools*. Report for Qualifications and Curriculum Authority. London: QCA.

Martin, C. (2008) *Primary Languages. Effective Learning and Teaching*. Exeter: Learning Matters.

Maynard, T. (ed.) (1997) *An Introduction to Primary Mentoring*. London: Cassell.

McLachlan, A. (2009a) *French in the Primary Classroom*. London: Continuum.

McLachlan, A. (2009b) Modern languages in the primary curriculum: are we creating conditions for success? *Language Learning Journal*, 37(2): 199–219.

Moyles, J. and Stuart, D. (2003) Which school-based elements of partnership in initial teacher training in the UK support trainee teachers' professional development? In *Research Evidence in Education Library*. London: EPPI Centre, Social Science Research Unit, Institute of Education.

Muijs, D., Barnes, A., Hunt, M., Powell, B., Arweck, E. and Lindsay, G. (2005) *Evaluation of the Key Stage 2 Language Learning Pathfinders*. Nottingham: DfES.

Nuffield Languages Inquiry (2000) *Languages: The Next Generation*. London: The Nuffield Foundation.

Ofsted (2002) *The Curriculum in Successful Primary Schools*. HMI 553. London: Ofsted Publications.

Ofsted (2003) Primary modern foreign languages in initial teacher training: A survey. Available at http://www.ofsted.gov.uk

Ofsted (2005) *Implementing Languages Entitlement in Primary Schools: An Evaluation of Progress in Ten Pathfinder LEAs*, available at http://www.ofsted.gov.uk/assets/3948.pdf

Ofsted (2008) *Primary Languages in Initial Teacher Training*, Reference No: 070031, London: Ofsted, available at http://www.ofsted.gov.uk/assets/Internet_Content/Shared_Content/Files/2008/jan/itt_primarylanguages.pdf

Pachler, N. and Field, K. (2001) *Learning to Teach Modern Foreign Languages in the Secondary School*. London: RoutledgeFalmer.

Partridge, J. (1994) Metalinguistic awareness and learning a foreign language, *Primary Teaching Studies*, 8: 64–9.

Pinter, A. (2006) *Teaching Young Language Learners*. Oxford: Oxford University Press.

Powell, B., Wray, D., Rixon, S., Medwell, J., Barnes, A. and Hunt, M. (2000) *Analysis and Evaluation of the Current Situation Relating to the Teaching of Modern Foreign Languages at Key Stage 2 in England*. London: Qualifications and Curriculum Authority.

QCA (Qualifications and Curriculum Authority) (2000) *Curriculum Guidance for the Foundation Stage*, Ref: QCA/00/587. London: QCA.

Roberts, C. (1997) The year abroad as an ethnographic experience, in M. Byram (ed.) *Face to Face: Learning 'Language-and-Culture' through Visits and Exchanges*. London: CILT.

Rowe, J. and Campbell, A. (2005) An investigation into effective school-based tutoring of Primary Modern Foreign Language Trainees. TTA ITT Research and Development Project, available at www.ttrb.ac.uk/attachments/0cc8c97f-afe0-4fad-8bc7-b953ca198379.doc

Schön, D. (1983) *The Reflective Practitioner: How Professionals Think in Action*. London: Temple Smith.

Schools Council (1966) *French in the Primary School*, Working Paper No. 8. London: HMSO.

Sergiovanni, T. (2001) *Leadership: What's in it for Schools?* London: RoutledgeFalmer.

Simon, B. (1991) *Education and the Social Order 1940–1990*. London: Lawrence & Wishart.

Stenhouse, L. (1975) *An Introduction to Curriculum Research and Development.* London: Heinemann.

Street, B. V. (1993) Culture is a verb, in D. Graddol (ed.) *Language and Culture.* Clevedon: Multilingual Matters.

Taeschner, T. (1991) *A Developmental Pyscholinguistic Approach to Second Language Teaching.* Ablex, NJ: Norwood.

Teacher Training Agency (1998) *National Standards for Subject Leaders.* London: Teacher Training Agency.

Training and Development Agency for Schools (2007) *Professional Standards for Teachers.* London: TDA.

Whitaker, P. (1993) *Managing Change in Schools.* Buckingham: Open University Press.

Wood, D. (1998) *How Children Think and Learn.* Oxford: Blackwell.

# Index

Agency 5, 179
Alexander, R. 5
ALL 19, 110
Assembly 76, 111, 170, 172
Assessment 13, 82–99, 147
Assessment for learning 82–3
   feedback 82, 84, 90
   learning intention 88
   'no hands up' 85, 86
   peer assessment 88–9
   self assessment 88–9, 97
   success criteria 88
   summative assessment 83, 98
   traffic lighting 86
   thumb tool 87
   2 stars and a wish 87–8
Assessment plan 96–8
Asset Languages 90–1
Attainment Targets 31, 38–40, 51, 89–90,
   95–6, 113
   exceptional performance 39
Attitudes
   learning 2
   pupil 8, 10, 108, 117, 122, 148
   teacher 10, 14, 15, 24
Authentic
   contexts 169, 173
   materials 111
   purpose 38, 44, 61, 67, 71, 112

Barrett, M. 173
Beaton, R. 68
Best practice
   planning 31, 58
   teaching 109, 145, 149, 158–9
Big Books (see also reading) 112
Black Box (see also AfL) 83–5
Black, P., Harrison, C., Lee, C., Marshall, B.
   and Wiliam, D. 83–4
Blended learning/skills 60, 63, 66,
   89–90
Bolster, A., Balandier-Brown, C. and
   Rea-Dickins, P. 117
Brighouse, T. and Woods, P. 176
British Council 58
Building capacity 14, 100–1, 109, 119,
   184
Burrows, D. 106

Burstall, C., Jamieson, M., Cohen, S. and
   Hargreaves, M. 6–9, 116–8
Byram, M. 178

Cable C. et al 61
Cameron, L. 26–7
Challenge 39, 66, 86, 179
Child language development 26–9
Citizenship 41, 175
Clarke, S. 89, 99
Class management 49, 71
Cochran-Smith, M. and Lytle, S. 176
Collaboration 3, 57, 98–9, 117, 125,
   164–5
Common European Framework 25, 90,
   162
Communication 60, 72–3, 155
Community of practice 28–9, 116, 160,
   163
Comprehensible input 60
Consolidation 122
Continuity (see also transition) 102,
   116–30
Council of Europe 10, 90, 94
Cross-curricular teaching and learning
   3, 13, 21, 23, 31, 33, 36–7, 41–2,
   48–50, 51–2, 61, 64, 77–8, 111–2,
   140, 155
Culture 170
   cultural awareness 11, 17, 21, 23–4, 49,
   147, 160, 167–9, 170, 174–5
   cultural competence 23
   cultural symbols 24
Curriculum map 48, 52
Curtain, H. and Pesola, C.A. 23

Dart, B., Boulton-Lewis, G., Brownlee, J.
   and McCrindle, A. 150
Dearing, R. and King, L. 11, 116–7
DCSF 1, 61, 90
Development
   child 2, 3, 22, 29, 81
   cognitive 28
   curriculum 10
   educational 6, 11, 15, 23
   intercultural competence 24
   language skills 9, 11, 26–9, 78, 79,
   178

Development (*Cont.*)
   professional 20, 21, 24, 29, 55, 100,
      104–5, 107–10, 131–9, 145, 148–9,
      151, 159, 160, 167, 169, 174, 176,
      177, 179
   social 28
   teacher 2, 17
Dewey, J. 148, 149
Differentiatiated; differentiation 35, 43, 45,
      47, 48, 50, 51, 61, 67, 79, 80, 96, 112,
      126, 154, 156,
Discontinuities (see also transition) 85,
      118–9
Display 37, 41, 62, 64, 75, 76, 77, 78, 81,
      107, 153, 170, 174
Doyé, P. 23–4
Driscoll, P. and Frost, D. 10, 19
Driscoll, P., Jones, J. and Macrory, G. 3, 12,
      20–1, 102
Driscoll, P., Jones, J., Martin, C.,
      Graham-Matheson, L., Dismore, H.
      and Sykes, R. 117, 138

EAL 78–80
Earley, P. and Weindling, D. 106
Effective
   Practice 17–30, 99
   Teaching 80
   Planning 32–59
Embedding 71, 73–6, 152–3
Error correction 67–8, 70, 88
European languages portfolio (ELP) 93–4
Every Child Matters 3, 11, 17–8
Exploring language 62

Feedback (see also AfL) 82–100, 139, 143
   mentoring 131, 133–4, 137–9, 142, 144,
      163
Foreign language assistant 56–8
Formative assessment (see AfL)
Funding 10, 15

Galton, M., Gray, J. and Rudduck, J. 85,
      118
Games
   use of 35, 70, 80, 111, 113, 123, 156, 166,
      168,
Gifted and Talented 25, 107
Grammar 68, 69, 71, 74, 80, 81

Hall K. and Hardin, A. 61
Harris, A., Day, C., Hopkins, D., Hadfield, M.,
      Hargreaves, A. and Chapman, C. 101

Hawkins, E. 7, 9, 10, 25, 72
Heath, H. 150
Holistic approach 59, 76, 77, 97
Holly, M. 149
Homework 74–5, 152–3
Hopkins, D., Ainscow, M. and West, M. 2, 3
Hopkins, D. and Jackson, D. 109
Hoy, P. 9–11

ICT 22, 25, 37, 41, 49, 77, 104, 113, 141,
      168,
Inclusive practice 60, 72, 77
Independent learning 3, 4, 166–7
Intercultural competence 24, 174
Intercultural understanding 24, 41–2, 170
International contexts 14
   links 171

Jones, J. 4, 88, 117, 119
Jones, J. and Coffey, S. 85, 117
Jones, J. and Wiliam, D. 4

Kirsch, C. 24, 60
Kramsch, C. 24
KS2 Framework 13, 21, 31–4, 36, 56, 60,
      109, 147–8
Knowledge about Language (KAL) 28, 32–4,
      62

Language aquisition 22, 26, 60, 177
Language awareness 62
Languages ladder 90–3, 124
Languages policy 15, 100, 109, 110–4, 126,
      137, 147
Language skills 24–5
   listening 66, 67, 152
   speaking 27, 51, 138
   reading 34, 63, 74, 75, 76, 163
   writing 63–4, 125, 152, 164
Language Learning Strategies (LLS) 4, 32–4,
      38
Lazaro, C. M. 7
Leadership 15
   distributed leadership 106, 114
   school leadership 12, 103, 130
   shared leadership 101
   subject leadership 100–115, 147, 178
Learning groups 73, 89, 98–9
Learning objectives 4, 32, 34, 36, 43, 44,
      48–9, 54
Learning strategies 32, 38, 61, 93
Learning support assistant 55–7
Lesson plan (see planning)

Lifelong learning 2, 4, 6, 29, 90, 93, 116, 179
Lightbown, P. and Spada, N. 26
Literacy 1, 8, 10, 26, 36, 48, 49, 57, 60, 61, 62, 64, 65, 66, 68, 69, 74, 76, 77, 78, 79, 80, 125, 140, 142, 166–7, 168
  the KS2 Framework for Languages 4, 33, 36, 37, 154
  links 12, 13, 14, 21, 41, 47, 147, 155
  the National Literacy Strategy 12, 112
  Primary National Strategy 3, 32, 154
  the Standards for QTS 127
Loughram, J. 178
Low, L. 101

Macrory, G. 72
Macrory, G. and McLachlan, A. 2
Management 105, 114
Martin, C. 12, 98, 101
Maynard, T. 132, 139
McLachlan, A. 4, 10, 24, 76, 101–2
Mentor development and skills 131–44
Metalinguistic awareness 26, 28, 61, 65
Monitoring (see also assessment) 98, 115
Moyles, J. and Stuart, D. 132
Muijs, D., Barnes, A., Hunt, M., Powell, B., Arweck, E. and Lindsay, G. 4, 12

NACELL 30, 93, 94
National Languages Strategy 1–5, 11
Networks 109
NFER evaluation (see Burstall)
Nuffield 7, 11

Observation 129, 138–44, 147–8, 153–8
Ofsted 21, 24, 48, 54, 61, 70, 83, 85, 102, 131, 145, 158
Online community 29–30
Oracy 4, 10, 14, 32–3, 37, 47, 49, 60–1, 65–9, 78, 79, 140, 154
Organizational learning 106
Overseas professional placement 160–175

Pachler, N. and Field, K. 22
Partridge, J. 28
Peer observation 159
Pinter, A. 27
Planning 31–59
  lesson plan 43, 51
  lesson planning 42–55
Powell, B., Wray, D., Rixon, S., Medwell, J., Barnes, A. and Hunt, M. 12
Presentation and practice 68–70

Professional learning 104–6, 148, 161, 176–7
  Inset 105
Progression (see also transition) 4, 12–13, 31–2, 35, 37–9, 116–129, 40, 48–50, 82, 84–5, 89–90, 94, 98, 109, 113, 158, 177
  in trainees' development 136, 162
Pupil language 68, 72–3, 173–4
Pupils attitudes 8, 119–22, 173

QCA 34–8, 451, 54, 56, 109, 112–4, 158
QTS standards 22–3, 140–3
Questions
  Q/A 69, 86
  Rich questions 85–6

Real world learning 169, 173
Record of achievement 96, 127
Recording 94–6
Reflection/reflective practice 148–53
  critical reflection 148–9
  reflection in action 149
  reflection on action 149
  reflective journal 150–1, 165–7
Related learning content (see cross-curricular) 71
Research 121, 177–9
  'inside-out' 177
  teacher as researcher 178–9
Risk management 172
Roberts, C. 170
Rowe, J. and Campbell A. 131, 133, 136

Savoirs (les 4 savoirs) 175, 178
Schemes of Work 25
Schön, D. 149
School experience 145–59
School experience journal (see reflection)
School improvement 2, 3, 109, 176, 177
School Improvement Plan (SIP) 15, 102, 109, 147
School placement 135–7
School routines 73–6
School trips 29, 169–74
Secondary school 121–2, 124, 128–9
Sequencing 73
Sergiovanni, T. 101
Sharpe, K. 19
Simon, B. 6, 7, 151, 153, 165
Skills audit 106
Specialist Language College (SLC) 13, 14, 102

Stenhouse, L. 7, 149
Strategic language learners 68, 119
Street, B. V. 170
Subject knowledge 1, 14, 17, 19, 20–4, 25–6, 29, 30, 50, 105, 109, 132, 148
Subject mentor 131–44
Succession 102
Sustainability 10, 14, 101–2, 126–7

Taeschner, T. 28
Target language, use of 20, 21, 24, 28, 29, 34, 39, 61, 64, 65, 66, 68, 70–3, 76, 77, 78, 79, 80, 89, 100, 112, 132, 138, 151–5, 162–3, 170, 177
Targets 82, 144
TDA 19, 25, 161–2
Teacher competence 14, 17, 20, 21
Teaching assistant (see also Learning support assistant) 55–6

Teaching & Learning Strategies 56, 60–81
Team teaching 125
Teamwork 101
The National Languages Centre (CILT) 19, 29
Timetabling 12, 103
Transformational learning 170, 175
Transition 13, 95, 117–30
    transition plan 126–8
    pupils' views 119–22, 130
TTA 103, 108

Video conferencing 14, 174
Vision 105, 110, 134
Vocabulary 25, 29, 66, 67, 71, 92, 112–3, 123, 125, 127, 140, 152, 156, 158, 163

Whitaker, P. 101, 105, 106
Wood, D. 80